GASLIGHTING
How To Drive
Your Enemies Crazy
by Victor Santoro

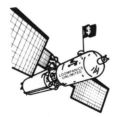

Loompanics Unlimited
Port Townsend, Washington

Gaslighting: How To Drive Your Enemies Crazy
© 1994 by Victor Santoro

Cover by Jim Blanchard

Published by:
Loompanics Unlimited
PO Box 1197
Port Townsend, WA 98368
Loompanics Unlimited is a division of Loompanics Enterprises, Inc.

ISBN 1-55950-113-8
Library of Congress Card Catalog 94-75742

Contents

INTRODUCTION

"Gaslighting" is a systematic array of techniques that destroys your target's mental equilibrium, self-confidence, and self-esteem, and is designed to drive your target nuts. Gaslighting is not conventional harassment or physical destruction, but highly refined and subtle psychological warfare.

Relatively crude harassing tactics, such as sending him magazine subscriptions and having his utilities turned off, make it unequivocally clear to the target that he's under attack by someone else. Harassment techniques are now well-known, and this has made it easier to construct defenses against them. Harassment may also turn the sympathies of the target's friends and associates in his favor.

Gaslighting is far more subtle, because most of the techniques never clearly point to a malevolent or vengeful other party. The hapless target never suspects that things are being done to him; he comes to believe he's doing them to himself! Gaslighting destroys his self-confidence and makes him doubt his competence and sanity. Other tactics are designed to alienate him from his family members, neighbors, associates, fellow employees, and even his employer!

2

The term "Gaslighting" comes from the 1944 Hollywood movie, *Gaslight,* starring Charles Boyer, Ingrid Bergman, and Joseph Cotten. In the movie, Charles Boyer tries to convince his wife that she's going insane by contriving incidents designed to make it appear as if she's forgetful, disoriented, and confused. As Ingrid Bergman played a Victorian housewife, Boyer's evil character had total control over her environment, and was able to use the force of his personality to convince Bergman that she had inherited bad genes from her mother, who had died insane.

In that limited Victorian environment, without electricity, telephone, radio, television, and E-Mail, the techniques available were very few. Boyer hid some of her possessions, to make it appear that Bergman was becoming acutely forgetful. Room lighting was by gas, which provided an opportunity for devious mind-damaging. Boyer would sneak into the attic, for example, to rummage among the goods stored in it, and turn on the gaslight, which would cause the pressure to drop in the bedroom below. Ingrid Bergman became so psyched-out that she thought she was imagining the dimming of the light in her room.

Today, it's possible to employ a variety of methods to destroy someone's self-confidence and emotional equilibrium. Everyday life is so complicated that it provides many avenues of attack. We can take advantage of modern technology to strike at the target simultaneously from several directions. We can convince the target that he keeps losing things, and that his memory is slipping disastrously. Gaslighting also destroys the target's credibility with his relatives, associates, and fellow employees. We can seriously impair his vocational and social relationships, alienating him from his family and friends. Gaslighting serves as a tool of attack, as well as defense against other people's unethical behavior.

Some reckless people have gaslighted their rivals and enemies by putting a psychedelic drug such as LSD or mescaline in their food or drink. Unfortunately, drugs show up on blood tests, a very good reason for avoiding their use. These extremes, which can get you in serious trouble with drug enforcement officers if you try to buy or administer illegal drugs, are unnecessary. As we'll explain, you can gaslight someone with commonly available and perfectly legal materials.

Most of the gaslighting tactics explained here cost nothing to execute. A few require a modest investment, such as a magazine subscription, a bouquet of flowers, or the price of a few keys. None are overly expensive, so gaslighting is within reach of even the most modest budgets.

Keep in mind that not all gaslighting tactics described herein are suitable for all targets. Some simply won't work because your target doesn't fit the situation. Others will be inappropriate because they don't provide the exact effect you wish. Yet others will be out of the question because you lack the right resources. Still others will be wrong because they can harm innocent persons. You have to be inventive, and able to design the best blueprint for gaslighting your target.

Your mental alertness and ingenuity will be your most valuable weapons, because it's impossible to lay out every possible variant of every possible tactic in this book. At times, you'll have to improvise, adapting existing techniques to your special needs. Given the nature of human ingenuity, you'll probably invent a few new tactics, as well.

In this book, we'll use the term "gaslight" as a verb. The past tense will be "gaslighted," not "gaslit." Someone who practices gaslighting will be a "gaslighter."

This book will use the masculine pronoun almost exclusively, except in cases where a female is indicated, although obviously most gaslighting tactics are workable against both males and females. This may be "sexist" language, but it makes writing and reading easier when we don't struggle through awkward phrasing such as "he/she," "his and hers," etc.

Read and enjoy this, but take it seriously. Even if you have no target in mind right now, someone else might be planning to gaslight you!

Chapter One
GASLIGHTING
PHILOSOPHY

Gaslighting is a method of attack. The purpose of gaslighting isn't pure physical destruction, but destruction of your target's intangible assets: his confidence, self-esteem, and reputation. You accomplish this by delivering a series of mental hot foots to destroy his mental equilibrium, something also known as "mind-fucking." Some forceful gaslighting tactics will seriously disrupt your target's life, but leave him wondering what he's been doing to himself. If you plan your attack well, your target will soon become tense and anxious, wondering if he's losing his grip on reality, and certainly losing sleep over the strange experiences he's been having. His family, associates, and fellow employees will begin wondering if your target's going off the deep end. With just a little bit of luck, you can eventually reduce your target to a shapeless mass of shivering, quivering jelly.

Selecting Your Target

Gaslighting is a powerful method of reprisal, and to make it worthwhile, you must be very selective in its application. Gaslighting isn't a weapon to use against a clumsy or rude waiter, or an inconsiderate person who doesn't return your phone call. Don't waste your time trying to gaslight someone who flips you the bird in traffic, either. Frankly, if you take offense at such minor slights, you'll spend your life alienated from most people, because people aren't perfect, and sometimes give offense without malice. In other words, don't go around with a chip on your shoulder and don't be an "injustice collector." Save your strength for the significant issues.

Tactically, it's best to save your efforts for a really important target instead of dissipating them on minor annoyances. You'll be better off focusing your efforts on a target that really matters instead of trying to settle scores with everyone who rubs you the wrong way.

Gaslighting is for people who intentionally hurt you, with premeditation, and without consideration for your feelings or any attempt to make it up to you. The utterly immoral back-stabber is a prime target. An extreme example is the "best friend" who is porking your wife. Another is the fellow employee who tells your supervisor malicious lies about you behind your back. You may also feel inclined toward revenge against the bad-mannered and noisy neighbor who persistently plays his stereo late at night, and dismisses your requests to lower the volume.

Let The Punishment Fit The Crime

Gaslighting allows you to tailor your tactics to give your target the same level of mental anguish he's caused you. This is an extremely important point, because the main reason for gaslighting an adversary is to make you feel better.

We've learned a lot about victims and victimization during the Twentieth Century. Police officers quickly learn how victims react to being victims of crime. Victims often feel violated and powerless, and this is true whether the individual has suffered criminal victimization or been victimized in a way not punishable by law.

The worst aspect of victimization experienced is the fact that aggressors usually get away with it. The rate of clearance for burglary, for example, is about 13 percent nationwide. If you ever suffer burglary, the odds are overwhelming that the burglar will get away with it, and that you'll never see the stolen property again.

Although nobody keeps statistics on non-criminal victimization, it's painfully obvious that ruthless aggressors get away with it practically all of the time. The employer, for example, who blames you for one of his blunders and fires you for it, is almost invulnerable to reprisal. You can, in theory, take him to court, but this is a long and rocky road even if you win, and "justice delayed is justice denied."

Don't Be A Loser

The victim, aware of his powerlessness, often feels like a loser, and he is a loser unless he takes steps to inflict as much distress on the aggressor as he's suffered. Sometimes, the urge to take reprisal explodes in irrational violence. Watching the news, we hear about former employees shooting up post offices, restaurants, or workplaces because the stress of unfair treatment was too much for them, and they snapped. Unfortunately, such actions are clearly illegal, and the former victim loses a second time because he's prosecuted if he survives. Some commit suicide, unwilling to face prosecution. Their relatives suffer, as well, because the gunman is labeled as a "mad dog" and the person who caused the original problem is treated like a hero or victim.

If you've become a victim, the problem is to find a balanced solution. Doing nothing will leave you feeling helpless and even depressed. Over-reacting can cause more trouble for you than it's worth. Gaslighting is the happy medium, because it's flexible, allowing you to adapt your tactics to each individual situation.

Many crude harassment tactics are obsolete. Many periodicals demand payment with the subscription, to forestall spurious subscriptions. Ordering pizzas, flowers, or liquor for your target by telephone is much more difficult today, because suppliers ask for your telephone number and, in locales with "Caller I.D.," can check right away to ensure that you've given the correct number.

Unlike harassment, gaslighting works best when you're close to your target. It'll become obvious, as we study gaslighting techniques, that it's easier to devastate a close associate than a total stranger.

Progressive Planning

A fundamental aspect of gaslighting doctrine is that it's a progressive attack upon your target's personality first, followed by his social and occupational relationships. Unlike harassment, where you work from the outside in, gaslighting begins at the center and works out. The sequence of tactics is important, because if you were to mount a direct attack first, you'd run into a strong and fully functioning personality, able to resist the assaults.

For example, if you were to tamper with your target's e-mail as your first step, he'd be quickly aware that a malevolent influence was at work, and would be on his guard against further intrusions. Once he thinks that someone's out to get him, he'll be a much harder target to hit effectively.

This is why the first phase in any gaslighting program must be to create an aura of self-doubt, and to destroy the target's self-confidence. From this, it's easy to understand that gaslighting is more subtle than harassment, and requires a more delicate touch. It's very much like the difference between an injection of anesthetic and a blackjack blow to the head.

Basic Tactics

There are several steps in preparing a gaslighting campaign against a target. The first is to find out all you can about your target, to uncover points of entry into his life. The following list provides a minimal outline of what you need to know:

- ✓ Full name
- ✓ Home address
- ✓ Home telephone
- ✓ Marital status
- ✓ Spouse's name
- ✓ Number of children, if any
- ✓ Children's sex and age
- ✓ Other relatives
- ✓ Occupation
- ✓ Work address
- ✓ Work telephone
- ✓ Name of supervisor
- ✓ Names of fellow employees
- ✓ Spouse's workplace
- ✓ Hobbies and interests
- ✓ Motor vehicles owned
- ✓ License plate numbers
- ✓ Credit card accounts
- ✓ Bank account numbers

This basic information allows you to study your target's lifestyle and plan the best ways to cause him mental anguish and dislocation. Beyond the basics, it helps to know the subtleties of his relationships. How well does he get along with his family? His friends? His fellow employees? The more you know about him, the more ways you'll find to attack him. Let's explore this in detail.

Exploiting Opportunities

As important as the basic details is the psychological and social picture you find. Is your target normally tense and anxious? If so, he's already done part of your work for you, as it will take less effort to push him over the edge.

Does he shy away from people? Is he uncomfortable with fellow employees and neighbors? If so, look for the reasons, which may highlight a plan of attack.

Is he the company spy, or does he play company politics in a particularly cruel and ruthless way? Has he made many enemies at work, or does he have repeated disputes with his neighbors? Does he have many sins on his conscience, aware that many people he's hurt are waiting for him to stub his toe, and perhaps even give him a little push? It's important to remember that the more your target's associates and fellow employees dislike him, the more willing they'll be to believe the worst about him.

The greater the number of people who have it in for your target, the easier it will be for you to obtain help for your gaslighting projects. Make a list of his enemies, as well as his well-wishers, to provide a framework for recruiting accomplices.

Why his friends and well-wishers? Because if your target is truly a nasty, treacherous person, it's a sure bet that he'll alienate one or more of his friends with his traitorous tactics. A former friend, burning over a betrayal, will be eager to exploit the opportunity to avenge a stab in the back. As a close associate, he'll know some of the details that will open your target up to gaslighting.

Information is the first dimension; access is another. The greater your social and physical access to your target, the more you'll be able to do to him. This is in sharp contrast to techniques of harassment, in which you strike from a distance. The best situation is if you have both occupational and social contact with your target. This doesn't mean that he has to be a personal friend, and with some notable exceptions, you wouldn't be gaslighting a friend. You just need proximity and invisibility. If you work for the same company, and attend the same social gatherings, both serve as entries into your target's life. As a neighbor, you can observe your target and form a detailed picture of his schedule, interests, and lifestyle. These points of entry serve both for information and for action against him.

Let's look at the prospect of invisibility. If you work for the same company, you don't even have to be his peer. You can be a secretary or even the janitor, because to many people, janitors are invisible. We take them for granted, barely acknowledging their presence as they go about their work. Your target, evil and snotty person he is, will consider the janitor to be beneath his notice, and perhaps even beneath his contempt. Likewise, many of these unsavory persons consider a secretary merely as one who types letters, answers the telephone, and fetches the morning coffee.

As janitor, you may not be able to mix socially with your target, but one compensation is that you have legitimate reason for being in the workplace after closing time, and legitimate reason for collecting the contents of wastebaskets, which can be very revealing. Credit slips, canceled checks, notes and letters, envelopes, and other artifacts retrieved from the wastebasket can be gold nuggets of information.

Harassment is as subtle as a firing squad. Gaslighting's main element is stealth. Strike from the shadows, with a delicate hand, to keep the target unaware that he's the subject of a thorough campaign of disorientation and dislocation.

Psychological Pearl Harbor

Surprise is an essential element in planning an attack, whether a military knock-out blow or a psychological assault. Your target should not discover that he's under attack until your plan is well under way and it's too late for him to counter it.

This is why you should never display open hostility toward him. Revealing your grudge negates the advantage of stealth because it alerts your target to the prospect of hostile action from you, and makes you the prime suspect when things begin happening. It also helps greatly to allow time between the incident that provoked you to plan retaliation and the beginning of your efforts. This allows the incident to fade from his memory, decreasing the chances of his suspecting that you're behind his misfortunes. With some gaslighting tactics, allowing time to elapse is essential for success, as we'll see.

Best of all is to avoid revealing that you're even aware that your target has done you dirty. Knowledge is power, and keeping it to yourself multiplies its effectiveness. If, for example, you discover your wife cheating with your best friend, don't have a confrontation. Pretend to be fat, dumb, and happy while you plan your revenge.

An important tactical point is that you should take advantage of any social, occupational, or emotional proximity to further your plans. The closer you are to your target, the easier it will be to deliver a stab in the back.

Some gaslighting tactics are possible only when you pretend to be a close friend or confidant. Intellectual and emotional proximity allow you to get inside your target's head and inflict serious damage. In some cases, closeness is devastating.

Employing Accomplices

While many gaslighting techniques are designed so that you can use them alone, others work better with two people. In many cases, you'll improve your chances of success if you have a confederate or two to support you. This is especially true if you're conducting a whispering campaign against your target. A target may accuse one person of "having it in for him," but if he begins voicing suspicions of several people conspiring against him, he'll present an image of paranoia.

Plan your strategy to make fullest use of the "multiplier effect," when one event provokes a series of subsequent events that make your target's situation even worse without your having to contribute anything more. Provoking a confrontation between your target and his employer is a good example of the multiplier effect, because the personal interplay during a confrontation adds gasoline to the flames. We'll study many examples of the multiplier effect in the following chapters.

Make Your Own Luck

Life is full of surprises, which is why you should always remain alert to new opportunities. When you begin a gaslighting campaign, you won't be able to plan it down to the last dotted "i" and crossed "t". You may find unexpected opportunities presenting themselves, and you must be prepared to jump in and take advantage of them before they disappear. An example is when a fellow employee is absent. This provides an opportunity to search his desk or plant material in his workplace.

Sometimes, you can make your own luck by taking advantage of a fleeting opportunity. One tactic is to "borrow" his key-ring, if he leaves it within your reach, long enough to have duplicates made of his keys. These will be extremely valuable when you begin gaslighting him.

The tactics in this book are under various headings, depending on whether they produce disorientation, or provoke confrontations with family, friends, or fellow employees. Others lead your target's friends and associates to begin wondering if he's having a mental lapse. However, there's no way to place them all in neat pigeonholes, because tactics and effects overlap. Many will have more than one effect, causing the target to doubt his sanity while provoking an unwanted confrontation with an associate or relative.

This is why gaslighting tactics are so effective. Often, one tactic will have several side-effects, thereby enhancing its power. Learn to make the most of this for maximum disruption against your target. Remember that there is no defense against a well-planned and executed gaslighting attack.

Practical Preparations

If you think you may conduct a gaslighting campaign against anyone in the future, begin preparing for it now. Some practical preparations can facilitate any gaslighting campaign, no matter who the target may be, and these are worth doing well in advance to avoid having to scramble at the last minute.

Official stationery from government agencies and letterheads from several companies can serve various purposes, so whenever you have an opportunity, take a few letterheads and envelopes from the office of every company for which you work. If you visit other companies, or a government agency, and have the opportunity to take a few forms and documents from a secretary's desk or drawer, add them to your file. As we'll see, commonplace forms such as hunting licenses and vehicle registration forms enable you to use devastating tactics against your target.

Don't forget employment applications. These also have their uses, as we'll see.

Collect bars of soap and hotel stationery from several hotels and motels around the country if you travel. If not, ask a friend who travels to pick up a few for you, explaining that you're a collector. You'll have good uses for these later.

Locate several second-hand thrift stores in your area. These will be handy for purchasing used clothing that you can use for several gaslighting tactics.

A couple of pairs of latex or thin plastic gloves may be essential, if you intend to intercept your target's mail or enter his home. It's very unlikely that your fingerprints will pose any problems, but it's so simple to avoid leaving any that the precaution is worth taking.

Two more preparations involve items that may be illegal, so be extremely careful if you decide to obtain them. The first is a small amount of an illegal drug, which you'll use only for planting in your target's clothing. Never make an illegal drug deal yourself, because you might get busted, but if a friend of yours uses an illegal substance, scrounge a small amount and save it in a plastic envelope for future use. It's best never to store illegal drugs where you live or work.

The second item is a handgun. In jurisdictions with strict gun control laws, obtaining any sort of firearm can be very difficult. In other locales, such as most of the "Sunbelt" states, you can buy a handgun at a garage sale, no questions asked. Don't worry about the quality of the handgun. Just wipe every surface with an oily rag after purchase to obliterate your fingerprints. Wipe off any cartridges you load into it, then put it in a plastic bag. Store it in a safe place away from home, if handgun own-ership is restricted in your area. You'll have several opportuni-ties for its use later.

Storing contraband items requires forethought and caution. Don't do anything stupid, such as keeping it in a safe deposit box, because a box is traceable back to you. One way is to bury it away from your home and workplace. Another is to put it un-der a floorboard or behind a loose brick in an abandoned building, keeping in mind that someone might accidentally un-cover it. Still, it's better to lose your stash than suffer arrest and prosecution for its possession.

If you need to begin gaslighting someone right now, you'll have to cut corners. Look over the business letters you've re-ceived recently, as you can use some of these for forgeries. You type a letter of your own, and put it just below the heading, then photocopy the composite. The result will appear to be a copy of a genuine letter.

One last-minute preparation is to order a rubber stamp with your target's name and address. This will be useful when you're sending "mail" on his behalf. Obviously, pay cash for this, and pick it up in person.

Two Words of Caution

Some of the tactics laid out here, such as obstructing your target's mail, are illegal. This points up the importance of not getting caught, although prosecution is unlikely. An important corollary to this, worth repeating, is to avoid advertising your animosity towards your target, so as not to let him or anyone else know that you're carrying a grudge. A show of hostility can kick back at you by making you a prime suspect, so you have to learn and practice diligent self-control. Gaslighting requires a fine hand, to avoid detection both by your target and by the authorities. Otherwise, you could be getting into far more trouble than you plan for your target.

Throughout this book, we'll be working on the assumptions that you're an ethical person, and that your target deserves whatever he gets because he's a bad person. The other side of the coin is to avoid harming innocent people while dealing with your target. Remember that many gaslighting tactics have side-effects, and involve other people in minor roles.

There's a fine line between involving an innocent person tangentially and involving him to the point of harm. The postal carrier who delivers a bill to your target isn't likely to suffer. On the other hand, instigating a fist-fight between your target and a totally innocent person can result in physical harm or legal problems for someone who never did anything to offend you. By contrast, provoking a non-violent conflict between your target and his employer will hurt only your target, because his employer can take care of himself. Keep your ethics straight: that way, you'll continue to be a better person than the blackguard you've selected as a target.

Chapter Two
CAUSING
DISORIENTATION

The purpose of causing disorientation is to produce a profound feeling of self-doubt and loss of self-confidence. Spatial and kinesthetic disorientation are subtle, but the tactics you can use to convince your target that he's losing his memory, and perhaps his mind, are blatant and forceful. You can reinforce this by inducing the feeling that nothing works for him anymore.

These are subtle tactics, designed both to induce loss of self-confidence and to avoid letting him know that he has a dedicated enemy. During this first stage, you have to be very careful not to leave a signature by using anything resembling harassment tactics prematurely.

Gimmicking Clothing
and Personal Articles

If your target wears a hat, and you can find one just like it but a quarter-size larger or smaller in a thrift shop, you can make him wonder if his head is swelling, or if his skull is shrinking. It becomes very easy if your target's headgear is a baseball cap with an adjustable plastic backstrap, and he leaves it on a shelf, hat rack, or in a locker. Simply change the strap by a hole or two when he's not looking.

Unless your target wears very expensive headgear, it's worth the extra cost of buying a new hat, and aging it by wearing it, crumpling it, and rolling it in dirt, then cleaning it to match your target's hat. Once you've aged it to match your target's hat, you can begin substituting it to promote disorientation.

If your target wears inexpensive, off-the-rack clothing, you can confuse him by buying another jacket or two a size too small or large. Switch jackets when he's not looking. While you're switching the jackets, take an extra minute to look through the pockets of his jacket, and place anything you find in the appropriate pockets in the new jacket. This will negate any suspicion that someone with a similar jacket took his by mistake. If you find a key ring or wallet, this is a bonus, and we'll discuss how to take advantage of this find later.

If the target uses a cane, replacing the rubber tips to make it appear that he's getting taller or shorter is another way to disorient him. A telescoping aluminum cane or crutch is even easier to adjust for length, usually requiring only a screwdriver or wrench to loosen the bolt or nut. Use this tactic carefully, changing his cane length in small increments, so as not to make it too obvious.

Move furniture and other objects to disorient your target. The more subtle you can be, the better this technique will work. If you have access to your target's office or home, the worst thing you could do would be to rearrange all of the furniture in one move. Your target would immediately realize that someone had done it without his permission, and he wouldn't develop the creeping self-doubt that results from more subtle methods. He might even conclude that someone had played a malicious practical joke on him.

Instead, change one item at a time. Move a chair or lamp, or switch his paper baskets to the other side of his desk. If he has an adjustable chair, raise or lower it an inch. Next morning, your target may not immediately realize that something's out of place. Instead, a sense of unease and mild disorientation will creep over him as he tries to readjust to the changed surroundings. When he finally notices that something's different, it will appear inexplicable. After all, who would sneak into his office or home to move a lamp a few inches?

This works in other settings, as well. If your target's a machinist, purloin his micrometer, caliper, or calculator, and wait until he's given up searching for it. Then put it back in a slightly different place. During the interval, your target may have even accused another employee of stealing it, provoking a confrontation that will alienate him from fellow workers. When the tool reappears, he'll be doubly confused.

Swapping Calendars

If you work with your target and he uses his desk calendar to record appointments, an excellent way to disorient him is to obtain another calendar just like the one on his desk and switch them every couple of days. Your target will write in appointments, but when you switch calendars he'll write them in the second one. When you switch them back, the entries written in the second one will be missing, while he'll see others he'd entered previously. As the entries are all in his handwriting, he won't suspect that one of the calendars is spurious, but instead will begin to doubt his memory.

This can be devastating. If your target has a clear recollection of having written an appointment a day or two previously, and now finds the space blank, he's bound to suffer severe self-doubt as he finds his memory contradicted by the tangible evidence of a blank space.

Borrowing His Keys

Gaining access to your target's keys is important, because if you can "borrow" them for long enough to duplicate them, the consequences can be enormous. If your target leaves his key-ring on his desk, or on his chair, don't be shy about taking them as long as nobody sees you do it. The trick is to put them someplace else when you bring them back unseen, to gain the bonus of making your target think he can't remember where he left his key-ring.

Canceling Teller Machine Cards

If you have access to his keys, you may also have access to his wallet. If so, bring a powerful pocket magnet with you, and run it lightly over the magnetic stripe on the back of one of his ATM cards, carefully leaving the others alone. Next time he tries to use that card in an ATM, the machine will either reject or retain it. Either way, it won't work, and he'll have to obtain a new card, all the time wondering why his card died on him.

Vanishing Newspapers

If you live next door to your target, and he has the newspaper delivered, you can add to his feeling that nothing works for him anymore. If you can swipe his paper without risk, do it a couple of times each week. By itself, this is insignificant, but added to other things going wrong in his life, it will add another mental hot foot to psych him out.

The Bottomless Gas Tank

If you can get the keys to your target's vehicle, make a duplicate of each one, especially if there's a gas cap key. If there's an inside release for the gas tank filler cover, you only need the key that provides access to the vehicle.

Never siphon fuel from his tank, as your target would merely conclude that someone was stealing his gas. Instead, each night add a couple of gallons to his tank. Your target will begin to wonder when he's due for another fill-up. It will never occur to him that anyone would add gasoline to his tank, and pretty soon he'll begin to doubt his memory.

Caution: resist the temptation to add molasses, acid, or other adulterant to his gas tank. This is crude sabotage, and will only warn him that someone has it in for him, big-time.

The Spurious Sticker

Service stations usually put a sticker on the door frame with each oil change, giving the mileage or date when the next one's due. Remove this, substituting a similar one dated a couple of months or a couple of thousand miles later. Not only will this add to his disorientation, but delaying servicing will increase the wear on his vehicle without overt sabotage.

The Strange Vehicle

With access to his vehicle, you can carry over the same techniques you used in his office. These are especially effective if he's the only driver, or if he's the only one to have driven his vehicle that day. For example, if he drives to work, get into his car and move the seat an inch or two. If he has an adjustable steering wheel, readjust it slightly for him. If he normally leaves the window down a crack to let hot air out during the summer, crank his window up to the top. In winter, lower the window a crack.

Another piece of subtle sabotage has a long-delayed action. Open his trunk and let the air out of his spare. This is another example of untraceable sabotage that can have serious effects. When he needs his spare tire, he'll find it useless, and will end up taking it in for a check. Meanwhile, the lack of a working spare will cause him serious inconvenience, and he'll be kicking himself for not checking his spare tire regularly.

Don't do anything crude or obvious, such as leaving cigarette butts in his car ashtray if he doesn't smoke. You're unlikely to convince him that he has a second personality that occasionally emerges to have a smoke. Keep it subtle, and let him worry about why his foot has to reach farther to press the brake pedal, or why he forgot to turn down the window on the hottest day of the year.

The Dead Battery

Another way to convince your target that he's losing his mental capacity is to turn on his headlights while his vehicle's parked. This works only if your target normally drives with headlights on, commutes to work before daylight, or drives somewhere after dark. You simply unlock his door and turn on his lights, to run down his battery.

At work, you appear to be helpful, parking your car near his so that you notice his distress at quitting time, and to ingratiate yourself with him, you offer him a jump-start with your cables. After the second or third occurrence, you can suggest to him that his memory is slipping.

The Moving Car

Another disorientation tactic you can use if you have the keys to his vehicle is to move it a couple of times a week. When you see him park it at work, wait until he's inside the building and move it to another parking spot. When he emerges, he'll be dismayed to find it gone, the moment of panic replaced by puzzlement when he sees it in a place he doesn't remember leaving it.

To make sure he doesn't begin to suspect this is being done by a fellow employee, follow him to a supermarket or shopping center. Once he's inside, relocate his car a couple of rows away. If his home doesn't have a garage, and he parks his car in his driveway or on the street, move his car one night.

Begin this program slowly, relocating his vehicle once a week, and step up your campaign later. For best results, move it only one or two slots away for the first week, then increase the distance until he becomes convinced that his memory is as full of holes as the hull of the Titanic. A bonus is that your tactic can have repercussions, taking advantage of the multiplier effect. Two possible scenarios are:

1. Your target doesn't find his car where he left it when he comes out of a shopping mall. He reports it as stolen to police, and when a police officer arrives to take a report, he finds it two rows away. This is likely, because police officers have had many "stolen car" reports from people who were merely forgetful, and often take a quick tour of the parking lot to see if the vehicle is on the premises.

2. If a family member, most likely his wife, also drives the vehicle, relocating it can provoke a confrontation between them. He'll accuse her of not telling him she had parked the car elsewhere, which she'll deny. Despite the repeated de-

nials, he'll continue to find his car elsewhere, which won't improve his disposition one bit.

The Fake Key

Jamming your target's home or vehicle lock with a toothpick or super glue is nasty and effective, but it would be counter-productive for your purposes. Your target would immediately know that someone had played a nasty trick on him, and would be angry at whomever he suspected. Instead, do something that will leave him confused and disoriented.

If you have access to your target's key ring, obtain a house key that closely resembles his, then swap them. He'll work up a sweat wondering why a key that looks so familiar doesn't work in his lock. He will have to call a locksmith to straighten out his problem, and the expense will far exceed whatever it cost you to have the fake key made. You can do the same for his vehicle.

One quick and dirty way to do this if you can't "borrow" your target's key for more than a couple of minutes is to use a needle file to file a few thousandths of an inch off one of the key's teeth. This will make the key unable to open any lock for which it's been cut.

An even quicker way is to break off the tip of a pencil in his cylinder lock. This will jam the lock temporarily, but the pencil tip will crumble into powdered graphite as he continues his efforts to insert the key. As graphite is a normal lock lubricant, and not a foreign substance, even a locksmith won't find anything to indicate tampering.

If you have elementary locksmithing skills, you can take this a step further. Instead of substituting a key, remove the cylinder of his front door lock and replace one tumbler with a slightly longer or shorter one, so that his key will no longer work. If his front door key also works for the back door or the storage room, leave those locks alone. Your target will now have a key that works perfectly on every lock but the one on his front door. When he calls in a locksmith, and finds out that one tumbler in the door lock doesn't fit his key, this explanation will be incomprehensible and confusing.

Pledging To Charities

Various causes regularly hold telethons and other campaigns to solicit contributions. One often used technique is to encourage viewers to telephone their pledges. Public television stations solicit pledges one or more times per year. To make this work, you simply telephone a pledge in your client's name to every telethon you can. The campaign operators will send your target a letter thanking him for his pledge, and an envelope in which to mail his check. Your target, of course, won't remember pledging anything. If he has, by coincidence, pledged a sum to that charity, it will probably be a different amount, and he'll conclude that someone else made a mistake. When the collection request with the correct amount arrives, it will appear confusing.

Party Time

If you're lucky enough to be close to your target, you may be able to disrupt his plans for a social gathering. A few examples will illustrate some tactics you can use:

If your target orders pizzas to be delivered at a certain time, and you know the pizza shop involved, you can disrupt his plans by a follow-up call. Don't do anything crude, such as canceling the order. Instead, change it. Telephone the pizza shop and order a change in the number or types of pizzas, or the time of delivery. If the pizzas arrive an hour early, they will be cold by the time guests arrive. If late, your target will wonder where his pizzas are, and may have to try to explain their absence to his guests.

If the invitations were verbal, and you're one of the guests, you arrive an hour early, and insist that that is the time he told you to come. At this point, an accomplice can be very helpful, if he also arrives early and tells the target the same thing.

With an accomplice, you can be even bolder. Telephone your target a few days before the gathering and tell him that you can't make it, then show up anyway. Your accomplice arrives with you, and if your target mentions that he hadn't been expecting you because you said you weren't coming, your accomplice states that this can't be so because you had planned to share the ride and attend together. This version is even more credible and convincing if the story is that one of you is the "designated driver" who will avoid drinking alcohol, following today's practice.

A Matter of Taste

As a guest in your target's home, you'll have priceless access which you can exploit cleverly. Apart from copying his keys and other preparations, you can gimmick his condiments lightly, to make him think that his taste buds are deceiving him. One way to do this is a variant on the old trick of replacing the sugar in his sugar bowl. Substituting salt would be entirely too obvious, but adding a small amount, just enough to make his coffee taste slightly strange, is enough. Adding a teaspoon of sugar to his salt-shaker will also produce a vague off-taste, a suggestion that his senses are fooling him. This provides one more increment of sensory disorientation.

A light sprinkling of finely powdered salt in a container of ice cream will also produce an unusual taste. For best effect, make sure the container you adulterate is partly empty. If you tamper with a fresh one, he might just conclude that the manufacturer had produced a bad batch.

If your target is a dedicated coffee lover, you can tamper with his coffee blend to make it taste unfamiliar. Most supermarkets sell "gourmet" coffee blends, many with artificial flavorings such as mocha, vanilla cream, mint, or hazelnut. Add a teaspoon of one of these flavored variants to his canister of coffee and shake well to blend it thoroughly. Again, be discreet and add only enough to change the taste subtly, to avoid making it obvious.

If your target uses cologne or after-shave lotion, this provides another opportunity for increasing his disorientation. Obtain a bottle of another brand, similar in color but with a very different odor. Add a few drops to his regular bottle, using just enough to change the odor without making the change glaringly obvious.

TIP! Many cologne and after-shave bottles have narrow shaker openings, making pouring practically impossible. Obtain a plastic syringe with a nozzle that will slip inside the aperture of your target's bottle. You should not need the needle. Even in states that restrict the sale of hypodermic syringes, you can obtain plastic syringe bodies in pet stores, where they're sold as implements for administering medicine to pets.

Simple Addition

You can produce severe disorientation if your target is your roommate or if you have legitimate access to his home. If he keeps a half-gallon of ice cream in his freezer, substitute an almost full container of the same brand and flavor when his is almost empty. Likewise, add coffee to an almost empty coffee can. The only limitation you must observe is to restrict your tampering to things he uses exclusively. Do not, for example, put a fresh toilet paper roll in place of one that's almost finished.

Paying Back A Loan

This is one of the few tactics in this book that's absolutely fool-proof, because it will work with stunning effect every time. You approach your target and hand him a ten-dollar bill, thanking him for the loan of the money. When he appears confused, you gently "remind" him that he had, indeed, lent you the ten dollars the previous week. Your target won't be able to understand how he could have forgotten that he'd lent you the money, and it will be inconceivable that anyone would pay back money he didn't owe. The effect of this tactic increases if you have an accomplice who does the same thing to him the following month.

Christmas Cards

One way to cause your target to puzzle over the gaps in his memory is to send him Christmas cards from people he doesn't know. Have several accomplices sign Christmas cards with first names only, and mail them to your target without a return address. As return addresses on Christmas cards are much less common than on business mail, he's unlikely to think the senders wrote the cards by mistake, and will wonder which of his friends he's forgotten. Using very common first names, such as "John" and "Bill" will add to the confusion.

Adding a personal message to the bottom of one or two cards will enhance the confusion. A line reading, "How did you like the cuff-links?," or "Hope the shirt was your size," will have your target trying to connect the card with presents he's received, or wondering what happened to the gift mentioned in the card.

Old Army Buddy

If you know that your target was in the armed services, one way to make him ponder which of his old buddies he's forgotten is to telephone his home or office while he's away, give a name, and leave a message that you're an old army or navy buddy and that you intend to take him up on his offer to look him up if you ever got to town. You don't leave an address or phone number, explaining that you're just passing through at the moment, but will be returning in the other direction next week, and will try to contact him again.

The Phantom Acquaintance

Another way to convince your target that his memory is slipping requires an accomplice who has never met your target. To carry this out successfully, you must have solid information about your target, you must be a "friend" or fellow employee, and you must brief your accomplice thoroughly.

Your accomplice, Charlie, approaches your target at a business or social gathering and greets him warmly, referring to a meeting they had the previous week or month. Your target may at first assume that this is a case of mistaken identity, but your accomplice's next words suggest that they had actually met and had a conversation:

Charlie: *Hi, Harry, good to see you again. Did you catch any fish last weekend?*
Target: *Huh? I'm not sure we've met.*
Charlie: *Sure we did, after the sales meeting last week. You told me you were going up to the lake for the weekend.*

At this point, you approach to tip the balance:

You: *Hi, Harry, Charlie. I see you've met again. Harry, Charlie was really interested in your fishing, 'cause he fishes himself whenever he can get away.*

Reinforcing Charlie's acquaintanceship is crucial, as it makes it impossible for your target to ignore. With you insisting that you introduced him to Charlie, and Charlie's referring to his fishing trip, there's no way Harry can ignore this, or pass it off as a case of mistaken identity.

Canceled Appointments

Another way to give your target a mental hot foot and promote disorientation is to telephone him when he's out of the office or away from home, leaving a message with a fellow employee or with his wife that you won't be able to meet with him as agreed. Of course, you leave an unfamiliar name, to confuse him further. An additional twist, if you want to make him waste some of his time, is to leave a telephone number.

The number you leave is not just a number you picked at random, either. Copy the number of a pay telephone inside a store you know closes at six, and leave word that your target can reach you there any time after seven. You do not choose the number of a person or business, because there might be an answering machine. With a pay phone, unless someone remains late, there will never be any answer when he tries the number. If he tries to dial the number outside the hours you specified, the tactic will still be effective because he'll be forced to conclude that his wife or fellow employee copied the number incorrectly. This can provoke a confrontation, especially if your target believes that the call was important.

Occupational Insecurity

A major point laid out in the chapter on basic tactics is that the more you know about your target, the more effectively you can strike at him. No tactic brings out this point better than the fake employment ad.

If you know where your target works, exactly what he does, and if you also know that your target regularly scans the "help wanted" ads, this knowledge offers you a priceless opportunity to strike a blow at his peace of mind. The tactic is to place a classified ad for your target's job in the newspaper he reads. Be as specific as you can, listing the company and the exact position.

This works best if your target's position is unique in the company. He's not going to worry much if he sees an ad for assembly-line workers and he's one of 200 in that position. However, if he's the Purchasing Director, or Comptroller, he's on the hot seat. Note that this tactic will be terrifyingly effective if your target already feels insecure about his position, or has recently had a confrontation with the boss.

This is a perfect example of the need to remain alert to sudden opportunities. You may not have even considered a fake employment ad in your original plan, but if, for reasons entirely unconnected with you, your target has a heated, door-slamming confrontation with his boss, the opportunity this provides is too good to ignore.

The beauty of this plan is that, even if he confronts the situation squarely and asks his boss if he's going to be replaced, the most vehement denial will not give him peace of mind. Employers customarily don't provide an outgoing employee with advance warning. In some companies, fellow employees know of the impending execution through the rumor mill, but the victim finds out only when his supervisor takes him for the

short walk down the hall and furtively presses the final pay-
check into his sweaty hand.

The only explanation that would put his mind at ease is that
he's up for promotion, so of course the company has to find
someone to fill his slot. Fat chance.

Mail Games

One subtle way to make your target appear strange to corre-
spondents is to add an extra stamp to several of his letters as
often as you can. Extra postage works best if the envelope contains only one sheet of paper, making it obvious that the extra
stamps are wasted. This will make it appear that he used very
poor judgment in sticking on excessive postage. In fact, recipi-
ents of these over-franked letters may never mention it to your
target, although they'll privately think he's beginning to get
flaky. Even if one recipient does bring up the subject, this can
never point a finger directly at you.

Vanishing Mail

It's not a crime to put too many stamps on an envelope, but
tampering with the mail is very illegal, so be extremely careful
if you decide to make off with even one piece of your target's
incoming or outgoing mail. Intercepting his mail can be very
effective because it's hard to pin down responsibility for a letter
that never gets to its destination. You have to use this tactic in
moderation, though, to avoid the appearance of a deliberate effort by a persecutor. Let's take a look at a couple of scenarios
that illustrate how vanishing mail can be devastating:

*You know that your target is buying a new house.
You see an envelope from the real estate agent in his
incoming mail, and purloin it, carefully leaving all the
other mail. The application, or contract, never arrives,*

and your target will be contacting the agent, who will insist that he sent it. In some cases, the results will be inconsequential, as the agent can send another contract, but if time is of the essence, your target will lose valuable days before he realizes that something's gone seriously wrong.

Another:

Your target is in the habit of paying his bills by mail, and leaving them in the office outgoing mail bin. Riffling through the envelopes, you see one addressed to the local utility, the mortgage company, or the credit card company, and you take it. The result will be that your target will receive a notice of non-payment, and his credit rating can suffer. Your client may insist that he sent the payment, but the creditor has heard all possible excuses from delinquents and deadbeats, and won't buy his story.

This can be especially devastating if the envelope contains an auto insurance payment, and his policy lapses because of non-payment. Equally troublesome is a license plate renewal. Your target may be driving on expired plates before he catches up with the situation. If the cops stop him, they're unlikely to take his word that he sent in his renewal.

Yet another:

Your target signs a purchase order, contract, or other legal document, and you're able to obtain a copy of the original form. You pick his envelope from the outgoing mail, open it to retrieve that paperwork, type the relevant information on your spare copy of the document, and seal it in another envelope, without his

*signature. You mail it to the intended recipient, who
will then be forced to return the paperwork to your target with a request that he sign it, giving him yet another
mental hotfoot.*

Don't try to be funny and sign "Adolph Hitler" or "Hillary
Clinton" to such documents. This will only tip your hand, because both your target and the other party will know that a
prankster or more sinister influence is at work.

Switching Envelope Contents

Yet another way to produce aggravation and self-doubt for
your target arises if he mails several payments on the same day.
Using a wet sponge, you open two envelopes containing
checks, and switch them. Thus, the Internal Revenue Service
receives a check made out to the electric company, and the
electric company receives the IRS check. The electric company
will not accept the check made out to the IRS, which in any
case is likely to be excessive, but the IRS sometimes over-
stamps the payee with its own stamp, depositing the check as
partial payment and billing your target for the balance. This will
cause him extra problems with his checkbook balance. Again,
this is very unlikely to be traced to you because putting the
wrong check in an envelope isn't a terribly uncommon mistake.

The Missing Check

Another way to cause your target a delayed-action mental
hotfoot presents itself if you have access to his checkbook. Remove one check from near the bottom of the pad, tear it up, and
flush it down the toilet. When your target gets to the one below,
he may notice the skip in number sequence, and begin racking
his brain trying to remember a check he's sure he must have
written but forgot to record. If he doesn't notice the gap, he may

get a reminder if his bank lists gaps in check sequence on its statements.

Laundry Time

If you have access to your target's laundry hamper, note the contents and select a bright color from the items inside the hamper. Buy a package of dye the same color, and at the next opportunity, pour the contents of the dye envelope into a pocket of the apparel you've chosen. When this goes in the wash, it will appear as if the color has "run" to stain all of the contents of the washer.

The Bottom Line

A well-planned and forcefully executed program of psychological tactics can shatter your target's self-confidence. After a series of disorienting incidents, he'll feel as secure as the captain of the Titanic after the impact.

Chapter Three
BUILDING
PARANOIA

Paranoia, for our purposes, means a feeling of persecution, and is an important step in your program of psychological warfare. Promoting such a feeling can make the target's anxiety level shoot up to the ceiling, and when your target's tense and anxious, his judgment will suffer. The purpose is to build a diffuse anxiety which cannot focus on any individual, and especially not on you.

Note that if you're not too subtle about it, this can let your target know that one particular individual is out to get him, which is counter-productive. This is why you should reserve some of these tactics until you've already got him confused.

The main fact you've got working for you in building paranoia is that most people are already paranoid or fearful for very realistic reasons. Your target isn't the only hateful person on Earth. There exist many unfriendly neighbors and fellow employees, and some are predatory by nature. It's very realistic to be apprehensive about such people, just as it is to worry about the "crazies" in our society who open fire in a post office or restaurant. Working to enhance your target's paranoia is easy because the nature of our society is on your side. In any case, the dictum, "Paranoids have enemies too," works very well when you're gaslighting your target.

The Anonymous Note

One perfect way to build anxiety is to go out to the company parking lot and leave an anonymous note on your target's windshield. The note reads:

Attention: This is my spot. If you park here again, I'll slash your tires!

Unsigned, it provides no information regarding the identity of the writer. Your target may bring the note to the attention of the company's security department, if there is one, but will spend several days worrying whether his tires will be slashed in reprisal. The reason? Let's look at this closely:

The note indicates that someone thinks that the target parked in "his" spot, something obviously incorrect. This suggests that the writer isn't totally rational, and is extremely angry. The target may wonder if the writer is planning to do something to his car anyway, in reprisal.

A particularly effective variant of this tactic becomes possible if you have the keys to your target's car, because you don't have to create a phantom enemy. After he parks it, you move his vehicle to a spot assigned to someone else. There's no guarantee that the person offended will write a nasty note, but if you park the car in a spot reserved for the company president, the repercussions can be worse. Your target may receive a polite reprimand the first time, but after you relocate his car the third or fourth time, there will be fireworks. You can be sure that the boss will impose severities for this persistent and arrogant disregard of his prerogative. Your target's fervent denials will be useless, and may even aggravate the situation.

Whispering Sneers

Another way to foster your target's paranoia is to make it clear that people are, indeed, talking about him. For this tactic, an accomplice or two are essential. When your target is in the room, whisper to your accomplice, both of you looking in the target's direction to suggest that he's the topic of the conversation. Sneering while you whisper will suggest that he's being mocked, causing a very uncomfortable feeling.

It's necessary to use finesse to handle a possible confrontation, such as your target's turning on the people sneering and asking them if they're talking about him. A bold counter-attack will smash his self-esteem:

"What's the matter with you? Think you're important enough for people to talk about you? Getting paranoid or something?"

If you can get several accomplices to do this, the effect will be to diffuse his attention. Instead of focusing on one or two people who don't like him, he'll get the feeling that mockery and ridicule of him are widespread.

The Anonymous Accusation

Hitting your target with an anonymous accusation works best if he has a guilty secret, and you know what it is. An example is a married man's office romance. Leaving an accusing message on his voice-mail will make his blood pressure rise:

"Does your wife know what you're doing with Mary Jones when you take a three-hour lunch with her?"

Another scenario is the executive who regularly raids the petty cash:

"Does the boss know about those fake vouchers you've been filling out? What if he knew that you took the bus when you put in a chit for cab fare?"

These can create unlimited anxiety, because your target has no way of knowing how many people know his guilty secret. He does, however, know that people love to gossip, and if he has offended many people, can anticipate that they'll spread the news.

Let's look at some possibilities you can create even if you don't have any dirt on him. Some real-life situations generate suspicion, even if the person is totally innocent. Let's look at how you can create something out of nothing if your target is a doctor:

"Mrs. Jones was alone with you in your office for an hour last Friday. Does her husband know what's going on? What about your wife?"

This is particularly worthwhile because of recent scandals involving doctors who had sex with their patients. Another prospect is the clergyman or boy scout leader.

The scouting movement is particularly sensitive to this sort of accusation because adult leaders who molest members of their troops are not uncommon. This is why many scout troops guard against this by requiring that no adult be alone with a child, and adult leaders work in pairs or groups. Still, a scout leader may occasionally be unavoidably alone with a child for awhile, and if you become aware of such a case, you can fabricate a situation that suggests guilt:

"People have been wondering why you took Tommy Jones off by yourself last Friday. Do his parents know what you did with him?"

If your target doesn't have either voice mail or an answering machine, you can obtain the same effect with an anonymous note to his home or workplace. One tip: don't seal the envelope. Make it easy for the office snoop or a nosy relative.

Mind-Bending

It's remarkably easy in today's tense world to make someone think that people are talking about him, or have it in for him. Some people are predisposed to this outlook, and your tactics only intensify their suspicion and distrust.

Chapter Four
DESTROYING YOUR TARGET'S REPUTATION

Extending the concept of gaslighting involves not only making the target doubt himself and his sanity, but causing his relatives, friends, and associates to wonder about him as well.

The legal doctrine of an employer searching an employee's desk or locker for evidence of illegal activity is well established in this country. There are searches for stolen company property and illegal drugs. Certain companies have their security guards examine any packages or briefcases employees carry out the door. This provides the key to sabotaging your target's reputation, and lowering his esteem in the eyes of fellow employees.

Offensive Publications

If normal practice calls for a security guard to search every briefcase or package, smuggle a homosexually-oriented or bondage magazine into his briefcase. The guard's eyebrows will surely go up, and the find may become the subject of gossip.

Placing a perverted magazine in your target's desk can also be damaging. One way to arrange for it to be "found" is to have another employee find it. One way to contrive this innocently comes if a fellow employee asks you for a copy of a report or other paperwork. You can tell him that you lent it to Harry Target, and that it's probably in his desk. If your target is absent that day, he won't be around to deny that he has it, and the other person may look for it in his desk. Voila! He finds the magazine and the rumor mill begins.

Let's note that the publication need not be homosexually oriented. In fact, this might be useless in certain workplaces. In such cases a magazine covering bondage, whipping, or some other form of sadism may do the trick. In some places, inter-racial sex is politically incorrect. The key is that the publication must be contrary to the ethic or culture of the employer or fellow employees.

It doesn't have to involve sex. Someone employed by a lib-eral politician can suffer if you plant a copy of a right-wing publication in his desk. An abortion clinic employee will suffer embarrassment if a copy of a publication by the religious right surfaces in his possession.

If your target works for the American Civil Liberties Union or a similar organization, write to the Ku Klux Klan or the White Citizens' Council for information and a membership application form, using his name and work address. These or-ganizations use a boldly-printed return address on the envelope as a form of advertising, and anyone at your target's office who handles the mail will probably notice it.

Pure Rumors

Rumors, whether based on fact or pure fiction, can be very damaging, but they can also kick back at the person starting them. Instigating a rumor without ending up on the business end of a lawsuit for defamation requires discretion and a very delicate touch. Don't even try this unless you're sure of success.

The essence of defaming your target with a rumor is that it not get back to him. In many locales and workplaces, the dominant ethic is avoiding confrontations, and accusations will circulate behind a person's back without ever reaching him. One way to start a damaging rumor is if you have a female accomplice in the workplace or in your target's social circle. A second requirement, not absolutely essential, is that your target be unmarried.

Your female accomplice tells others in the group that your target has asked her for a date. She then relates one of several versions of what happened. You can really use your imagination in thinking up stories:

- Your target asked her to go to a funeral for their very first date, saying he enjoys attending funerals.
- He turned out to have kinky sexual tastes, such as whips and chains, or threesomes.
- He invited her to his home, where contrary to her expectations, they spent the entire time watching kinky sex videotapes.
- Your target tried to have sex with her, but was impotent.
- He was inexcusably rude and inconsiderate. After sex, she asked him when they would meet again, and his reply was: "Not necessary, my dear, I've already had you."
- He turned out to be secretly married.

The effectiveness of these rumors will be enhanced if your target is already thought of as a geek or jerk by his associates. They won't mention the rumors to him, but simply add the damaging allegations to their store of knowledge about him, while enjoying a few laughs behind his back.

There is another type of rumor, "disinformation," intended to get back to the target. Disinformation is the ultimate mind-game, designed to mislead the target, and we'll delve deeply into the tactics and uses of disinformation in a later chapter.

Notes on Toilet Walls

Writing a note on a toilet wall, previously considered a practical joke, now has more serious consequences if you add your target's name and telephone number to them. One man was arrested after someone noticed a note written on the toilet wall in a K-Mart. The note invited boys to call a telephone number for sexual contacts, and a police officer with a young-sounding voice called the listed number. Police recorded the conversation, during which the writer incriminated himself, and arrested him on one count of "attempted" sexual contact with a minor.[1]

Writing notes on toilet walls won't get your target convicted, but it may draw the attention of the police to him. He may deny any perverted proclivities to a police undercover agent who phones, but that may not stop the investigation. Police know that pedophiles often seek out situations in which they come into contact with minors, and if your target is a teacher or scout troop leader, he'll receive close scrutiny from the sex crimes detail because he fits the profile of a sex offender.

Any close police investigation causes ripples. Police officers who interview friends and neighbors may request that they keep the interview confidential, but some people can't resist the temptation to gossip about anything involving scandal. More importantly, your target's employer, if interviewed by police, may hold it against him. It doesn't matter at all if the police investigation "clears" your target. Both police and employer will probably assume that, although no hard evidence surfaced this time, the target's probably got something to hide.

If he's a teacher without tenure, his contract may not be renewed next year. If in another occupation, he may be on the execution list for the next down-sizing. Whatever else may happen, promotion will henceforth be out of the question.

Naughty Magazines

If your target has an office with a waiting room, the odds are overwhelming that he'll have magazines on a table for his clients' perusal. "Salting" a few naughty publications among the legitimate ones will raise eyebrows.

An architect, for example, is likely to have a stack of architectural publications laying on the table. A few sexually-oriented magazines, the nastier the better, under the top ones will soon come to the surface.

This can be devastating if your target's occupation is one that demands rigorous morality. In some locales, nobody cares if an architect or interior decorator they hire is homosexual, but a pediatrician or clergyman would be sorely embarrassed if his patients or members of his congregation were to discover publications that called his morality into question.

How do you reinforce the impact, and make it impossible for your target to deny that the publications are his? It's very simple. You buy white stick-on labels at a stationery outlet and type your target's name and address on them before sticking them on the publications obtained from an adult or sex shop.

To cause him problems at home, if he's married, just buy him a subscription to a raunchy magazine, the sort found only in adult bookstores. Don't bother with *Playboy* or *Penthouse*, even though these have subscription cards that allow you to pay later, unless his wife is very puritanical. The really raunchy mags require the subscriber to enclose payment with his order, so this will cost you twenty or thirty dollars. The result will be worth the money!

Yet another way to cause your target severe embarrassment with his neighbors is to fake a subscription for him. You buy a homosexual or sadism magazine at an adult shop, type a white label, and stick the label to a plain brown envelope. Before dropping the envelope in the mailbox, you tear it open enough so that anyone picking it up can see the type of publication it contains.

The key to this tactic is the label. You type your target's name correctly, but use the address of a neighbor several houses away. If the mail carrier doesn't know everyone on his route, and delivers strictly according to the address, the envelope will end up in the neighbor's mailbox. The rest is inevitable.

This will also work if you address the envelope to your target's workplace, as long as you make sure to tear the envelope. When you do this, it doesn't matter what sort of work your target performs, or if he has a secretary or an office. Several fellow employees will see the raunchy magazine, and the news will spread.

Yet another way to produce this result is to send letters requesting their catalogs to various firms advertising in raunchy magazines. Provide your target's name and address, and sign his name, adding the statement, "I am over 21." Ads in such publications are for sleazy cross-dresser clothing, leather goods, dildoes, vibrators, cock-rings, tit-clamps, and other raunchy sexual paraphernalia. Not all catalogs come in plain brown envelopes.

Condoms and Other Items

Planting condoms where they're likely to be found by your target's fellow employees, girlfriend, or wife can be devastating. You have to choose your target judiciously, however. A bachelor would probably not be embarrassed if a fellow employee were to see a box of condoms when he opened his desk drawer. However, a wife is another matter, especially the wife of a doctor or clergyman. Planting condoms can be very easy in some instances.

In the southern states, motorists often leave a window open a crack during the summer months, to let out the hot air, when they park their cars. A condom will easily slip through the crack. The method is to slip a condom through the passenger's side window, if it's open, as it won't work as well on the driver's side. If the target's wife notices the condom on the seat or floor, she'll have some pointed questions to ask him! A used condom will have an even better effect!

Anyone who leaves his car unlocked leaves himself open to more raunchy tactics. Leaving a well-worn and smelly bra in the back seat is one way of provoking accusatory questions from your target's wife. Dirty panties, poop stains and all, are even more spectacular.

If you and your target go on a business trip together, this provides a perfect opportunity for framing him. If you know that his wife packs and unpacks his suitcase, slip a bar of soap wrapped with another hotel's label in his bag on the last day of your trip. The wife will wonder why he told her he would be at the Holiday Inn in Dayton when she turns up a bar of soap from a Best Western in Chicago!

If you're determined to be raunchy, slip a pair of dirty women's panties into his suitcase just before the return home. His wife will get a big surprise when she unpacks hubby's case!

If your target calls on you to substantiate his whereabouts with his wife, back him up in the certainty she won't believe you. Many women believe that men stick together to cover each other's infidelities. You'll have had the satisfaction of sticking a knife in his back while appearing to support him all the way!

Instrument of Evil

The telephone offers an entry into your target's life which you can exploit with devastating effectiveness. The following tactics work better if your target's number is unlisted:

A male accomplice telephones your target's home at a time when you know his wife is out, and asks to speak with her. He doesn't give his name, nor a number where he can be reached, and acts embarrassed that the husband picked up the phone.

The second version works in reverse. An anonymous female telephones while the husband is out, asking for him, and hangs up abruptly after the wife answers. Sorry, wrong number!

This tactic is most practical if you're a neighbor, and can see exactly when your target or his wife leaves their home. Alternately, if you're a co-worker, you know when your target shows up for work. Otherwise, you either have to "stake out" their residence, which attracts unwanted attention, or you have to take the risk that the person you're calling will actually be home.

A very devastating telephone technique holds absolutely no risk for you, and works every time. If you know that your target's having an affair, discreetly shadow him, and when he's almost home, dial his number. Hang up the moment his wife answers. This ensures that his wife will be awake when he enters, and aware of how late he arrived. If he'd promised to be home early, and depended on her being asleep when he finally crawled into bed, this technique will blow his plan sky-high. If he's stinking drunk upon his return home, so much the better.

Swingers' Clubs

Employing this tactic illustrates the need to know as much as possible about your target, his habits, and personal peculiarities. Using a swinger's club, or classified dating service, is one way to deliver a blow to your target's reputation.

The success of this tactic depends on your target's situation. If he's married and church-going, any proof of his adultery will have severe repercussions. In many environments, any indication of perversion will be a black mark against him. In some situations, the scandal will be serious enough to cause him to leave his job, or even to leave town.

You may discover, or merely suspect, that your target places or answers advertisements in "singles" magazines or publications devoted to sexual highways and byways. This may happen because he tells you, or you may see a copy of the publication in his desk, briefcase, home, or car.

If you do, don't rush to make others aware of his proclivities. Instead, note which, if any, advertisements he's marked, to gain an idea of his range of "interests." The next step is to place several similarly-worded advertisements in the same publication, using a blind address.

This can be a P.O. box, or a mail drop, but many publications today provide blind addresses for their advertisers. Responders address their replies to "Box xxx," care of the publication.

The nature of the reply depends on the type of publication, your target's proclivities, and the way you worded your ad. It may simply be a letter describing himself in very flattering terms, or it may be even more explicit.

Try to obtain a frontal nude photo of your target, which can be useful for other tactics. Trolling for photos depends upon how you word your ad. Some ads, in the more explicit publications, insist on a photograph, which, in this context, usually means a nude frontal photograph. Some state clearly; "No photo, no answer," or "Replies with photos get answered first."

With a little luck, your ads will pull in a reply from your target. The next step is to make photocopies of his reply, and copies of any photographs he may include. Finally, you mail a copy to his wife, employer, his neighbors, and his fellow employees to devastate his reputation.

Lost and Found

Bibliophiles often have stickers inside the front covers of each of their books, promising a reward to the person who finds and returns it. Naturally, the sticker lists the owner's name and address, and sometimes even his telephone number. You can employ this as a gaslighting tactic against your target. First, get a pad of stickers printed:

> *This book is valuable. There is a ten dollar reward for its return. If found, please return to:*
> *Harry Target*
> *1321 Bleep Avenue*
> *Sleazeville, USA*

Next, buy some raunchy porno novels with racy titles such as: *Hot Pants Homo, The Sadistic Japanese Submarine Captain, Paddling For Joy, Handcuff Lover, Going Down on Rick.*

The more perverse and nasty they are, the more successful your plan will be. For those of you totally unfamiliar with porno paperbacks, the era of plain covers is over. Today, most have explicit cover illustrations to capture a browser's interest.

Don't waste your money on new ones, though. Instead, buy used books from a second-hand bookstore, for economy. In any case, old and worn books will do better because they have the well-thumbed look. If some have pages stuck together, so much the better. Paste a sticker in each one, and leave the books in places your target frequents, and even a few he doesn't. Some good possibilities are:

- His workplace, to let his boss and fellow employees know the sort of trash your target reads.
- A park near his home, so that parents of small children can see the sort of material this man leaves around.
- On the sidewalk near his home, as if your target had "accidentally" dropped it there.
- Supermarkets and shopping malls in the neighborhood.

Someone finding such a book may return it when your target's wife is home alone. Although the timing is out of your control, the more books you seed throughout the area, the better the odds of this happening.

The Ghost Picture

If your target leaves his camera within your reach, borrow it for a couple of hours. Use it to take a close-up picture of an accomplice's genitals, then put it back where you found it. He will wonder where the extra photo came from when the pictures return from the photo-processor, and if his wife or girlfriend is the one who picks up the picture, she may get the shock of her life when she scans through the prints. In a small town, the chances of the photo processor or store clerk's knowing your target's family or friends are greatly increased. If he's a respectable and "happily married" man, a close-up shot of female, or even male, genitals will cause a stir. You can spend many happy hours imagining the scene that will take place when his wife asks him to explain that frame!

Likewise if your target's female, and married. Her husband will be very curious regarding the origin of that photo of a man's genitals.

Truth is the Best Defense

One absolutely terrifying way of destroying your target's reputation, or at least causing him severe embarrassment, is to publicize any of his dirty linen that appears in public records. This technique depends on factors totally out of your control, but if events move your way, you can make your target extremely uncomfortable.

Public records can be a gold mine of information. They can provide the raw material for destroying your target's reputation, credibility, and even his livelihood. If you keep an eye on the legal announcements page of your local newspaper, you'll regularly see legal notices regarding divorce, bankruptcy, and civil actions. If you're really determined, you can make periodic trips to the county court house to check records of trials and cases filed. This needn't be an aimless "shotgun" search, as you'll often get indicators of what to seek out. A rumor that your target's marriage is on the rocks, for example, will let you focus on divorce filings. If your target's vehicle has been repossessed, check out bankruptcy filings and civil actions, in case a creditor is litigating for payment of a debt.

Once you zero in on a court action, spend a few dollars for a transcript of the legal records. Make photocopies and mail them anonymously to those who will be interested in knowing, such as relatives, neighbors, and fellow employees.

Divorce isn't a scandal these days, but your target will feel very uncomfortable when he discovers that his friends and fellow workers have copies of the legal document, with all its details. Sending his boss a copy of a suit to collect debt will suggest that your target's wages may be garnisheed, and this can produce some uncomfortable moments.

This information will cause even more serious ripples if you send copies to all the companies which have issued your target credit cards, and all stores where you know he has credit accounts.

The more you know about your target's lifestyle, the better you'll be able to direct your search purposefully. A ladies' man, for example, just might wind up on the receiving end of a paternity suit. Sending copies of the paperwork to his fellow employees, neighbors, and clergyman will cause your target some uncomfortable moments.

One free-lance writer suffered when an anonymous malefactor unearthed a trial transcript in which he had served as an expert witness. Although this writer presented himself as an expert in law enforcement and the use of force, some years earlier he'd written for a sexually-oriented magazine, and the opposing attorney in this case asked him if he was also an expert on the female orgasm. The unknown malefactor made photocopies of the testimony and mailed them anonymously to other people in the field, causing embarrassment and loss of reputation to his target.

This is a good place to emphasize that cultivating sources of information about your target can pay big dividends for the time involved. If you work in the personnel office, you can find all sorts of leads regarding your target's lifestyle and potential problems. If the company provides medical insurance, you might find a record of payment for an alcoholism treatment program.

Heavy drinking in a locale with no public transport points the way to scrutinizing traffic court convictions. Publicizing a Driving Under the Influence (DUI) conviction can have serious repercussions. If, for example, your target took two weeks' "vacation" time recently, and you discover he secretly spent the time in jail serving a DUI sentence, letting his colleagues know where he spent his holiday will help your cause. Likewise if he spent time at an in-patient alcohol rehabilitation program.

Also cultivate personal sources. Make friends with your target's enemies and business rivals, who will be attuned to collecting dirt about him. A few well-chosen words, and maybe a few drinks, will elicit leads to damaging information. This can be explosive if it includes a criminal record.

A felony conviction, no matter how long ago, is always bad news, especially if his employment application form had a space for listing a criminal record and he left it blank. Finding a felony conviction will require knowing where your target lived in his younger years, but once you discover this, you can direct your search to court records in that area.

Notes

1. Mesa, AZ *Tribune*, October 6, 1993.

Chapter Five
PROVOKING CONFRONTATIONS

By this stage, you'll see the multiplier effect working for you. Gaslighting, producing wear and tear on your target's nerves, degrades his effectiveness. Another effect will be to make him edgy, and even paranoid. He's more likely to become involved in conflicts with others, as he follows the vicious spiral down to his destruction.

Protected Persons

If your target is female, or a member of a protected minority, you'll find it more difficult to carry out some of these tactics. If female, you cannot take advantage of anything sex-related, such as physical weakness. Employers today are very concerned about anything that can be interpreted as "sexual harassment" in court, which means that any problems you cause a female target at work should preferably be related to job performance.

Likewise for ethnic minorities. If your target is a member of a "black power" organization, you can't use this against him the way you would a Caucasian target's membership in the Ku Klux Klan. Exposing a minority target's incompetence on the job, however, will have several healthy effects:

- It will justify the feeling that your target is holding his job only because of "quota hiring," and not because of his ability.
- It will provoke resentment from fellow employees, which while not finding free expression, will kick back at your target in other ways. He'll be frozen out socially, and fellow employees won't offer him the help they might provide to others having a difficult time at work.
- Incompetence, if properly documented, can stand up in court as grounds for termination. Documentation must be solid, though, because the employer will have to be very careful before terminating a minority employee.

Creativity

We've already examined some ways to take advantage of existing conflicts between your target and another person. Now let's explore how to create some:

Both on the job and at home, your target is vulnerable to artificially induced confrontations with fellow employees, family members, and neighbors. The simplest way to set the stage for a confrontation is to report any derogatory comments your target makes about any fellow employee or neighbor to the subject of the discussion. If you have a witness, your target is in a weak position either to deny having made the comments, or to make a scene when he's outnumbered. An accomplice to back you up can be very helpful here, if you decide to become creative.

Let's note that some of the following tactics can backfire unless your target's self-esteem and standing with others are already very deteriorated. If you tamper with his e-mail, he'll know that he did not write a memo attributed to him if it's a total fabrication. On the other hand, if you make a subtle change in a memo he's sending, he might well think that he made an error.

In many real life situations, there is more than one potential target. This is all to the good, because it helps avoid the moral dilemma of provoking a confrontation between your target and an innocent person. In the workplace, your secondary target might be the owner's idiot son or the snitch. If there are two company spies in your workplace, for example, you can contrive situations that put them at each other's throats, to other employees' benefit. While the two snitches are fighting each other, they won't have time or energy to rat on other colleagues.

The Fine Art of Instigation

Sometimes you have to create the conflict from scratch. In other instances, you can take advantage of a pre-existing rivalry. For example, two people might be competing for a promotion or raise. This is a perfect beginning for you, and all you have to do is to make your target, or his rival, suspect that one is using unethical tactics against the other. What you've got working for you is the common knowledge that office politicing is a minefield, and rivals have used the dirtiest and most outrageous tactics against each other.

One way to pour gasoline on the flames of an office rivalry occurs if your office has linked computers, as in a local area network, and uses e-mail. Your target may be tempted to spy on his rival by sneaking a peek at his computer files. If you have access to your target's, or to his rival's, computer you can plant a file that will cause a serious problem. This takes the form of a nasty and inflammatory letter to the boss:

Dear Mr. Bigwig:

I know that you've lately become dissatisfied with Harry Target's job performance, and perhaps I can provide some enlightenment. Harry's been interviewing for other employment lately, as I've seen him bring in the **Daily Rag** *open to the help-wanted ads, and this probably explains his taking off without explanation in the middle of the day.*

I've learned that the reason he left his last job was heavy drinking. To date, I haven't seen any sure evidence of that here, but Harry's appeared a little unsteady at times, and we both know his judgment and attention to detail aren't the best. It might be a good idea to smell his breath.

He's also been insecure about his continued employment here, ever since he made that major error with the Gottrocks account, and had that argument with Gottrocks himself. He said to me that, if he ever had the opportunity, he'd "shoot that son-of-a-bitch like a dog."

With this attitude, it's hard to see him remaining with this company, much less receiving a promotion.

Sincerely,

Charlie Goodwill

In real life, it's unlikely that any employee would actually send such a memo to his boss, but to the person examining his computer files, this appears to be the draft of a letter Charlie is contemplating sending to Harry's supervisor. As such, it's very credible, because it depicts Charlie's inimical intent. To a target already quivering with paranoia, it will appear to be an imminent and grave threat.

Note that this is also effective without e-mail, in the form of a file on an ordinary computer disk. If Harry scrutinizes it and makes a copy to study the contents at leisure, he'll have an eye-opener. Harry will just assume that his rival intends to print it out as an ordinary memo.

The low-tech variant of this comes into play if the office doesn't have any computers, but your target or his rival regularly search each other's wastebaskets. You simply draft out your denunciatory letter, type it with a carbon copy, and put the copy in the wastebasket.

You can make this work even if your target doesn't rummage through his rival's wastebasket. You crumple the carbon, then flatten it out and attach the following unsigned note with a paper-clip or staple:

Hey, Harry,
I thought this would interest you.

This note and the attached copy will put somebody in deep doo-doo. Of course, the note is not in your handwriting, as you've had an accomplice write it. Preferably, the accomplice doesn't work for the same company and your target doesn't even know him. It would expose part of your plan if the target were to recognize the handwriting.

Yet another way to instigate a conflict, even in a low-tech office where the most sophisticated piece of equipment is the telephone, is to let the office gossip "overhear" your end of a conversation. You dial your home number, the weather report, or time of day, and after a greeting and a few pleasantries, carry on a conversation something like this:

> *"Yeah, Joe, I know, there's office politics here, too. Why just the other day one of the people, he's really a troublemaker, Harry Target, was saying that Chesley Goodman is a real jerk the way he botched up the Trimble account last month. Harry said if he'd been in charge, he could have done a much better job."*

The office gossip will almost inevitably repeat this, and when word gets back to Chesley Goodman, there will be an account to settle. There's only a slight risk that this will come back to bite you, because it's impolitic for the office gossip to admit that he was eavesdropping on a telephone conversation.

Another theme:

> *"There might be something opening up here for you soon. Harry Target was telling me the other day that he knows Chesley Goodman's on his way out. I'll let you know when that happens."*

Yet another rumor you can start the same way:

> *"I heard Harry Target's on his way out. They'll be canning him one of these weeks because he hasn't been producing."*

The effect of this can be serious if Harry Target has truly made several recent mistakes on the job and is, in fact, worried about his job security. The lame-duck employee tends to be a pariah in American corporate culture, and Harry may find his friends, if he has any, shying away from him.

Creating a conflict from scratch is more difficult than exploiting an existing one and requires good information, careful judgment, and a sense of timing. You must know both protagonists well enough to make an informed judgment regarding what will set off fireworks between them. This may be an ethnic or religious difference, or one of what is euphemistically called "lifestyle." Let's examine a few scenarios that cover various methods of operation to suit individual circumstances:

Percy is the owner's limp-wristed nephew, just out of college and working his first job with his uncle's company for twice the salary experienced hands are getting. Harry "Macho" Target is the shipping foreman, and you whisper to Percy that Harry hates queers, and that he'd better stay out of Harry's way because of his violent nature. You know that Percy makes up the payroll and covers other disbursements, and take advantage of your position in the accounting department to make one of Harry's expense chits or overtime slips disappear. When Harry comes to you to chase down his payment, you send him to Percy with this piece of advice:

"Just sweet-talk Percy and you'll get anything you want from him. He told me he thinks you're a real hunk."

Even one such encounter can make the sparks fly.

Homosexuality isn't the only issue that you can manipulate to provoke a confrontation. Let's look at a couple of ethnic entanglements:

Irving is the company snitch, and Harry Target is a noted brown-noser. You mention to Irving that Harry hates Jews with a passion, and if this doesn't produce immediate results, you place a bumper sticker on Irving's car. The sticker reads: "Hitler Was Right!" Then watch the fur fly. If Irving doesn't notice the sticker at first, you point it out to Harry, as if you're just showing him a joke. Next day, you scrape the bumper sticker from Irving's car and stick it on Harry's bumper, and run an old-fashioned "church key" can opener down the side of his car several times to get his attention.

The protagonists don't have to be fellow employees, although company politics often helps to season a conflict. You can create problems between neighbors, as well:

Harry Target is a Vietnam veteran, and like many Vietnam vets, hates Jane Fonda. You or an accomplice mention to him that Rick Sturdley, his neighbor, admires Jane Fonda both for her films and for her political courage in going behind enemy lines during the war. A couple of days later, you notice Harry's garden hose on his front lawn, and when you have the opportunity to do so unseen, you move it to water Sturdley's lawn. Go home, pull a chair up to the window, and watch what happens when Harry comes home.

You don't have to let it go at that. The odds are that the first incident will result only in an argument, but you can provoke follow-up incidents:

Harry comes home and sees his garden hose watering his neighbor's yard from his faucet. Turning it off, he angrily rings Sturdley's bell, and informs him that the next time Sturdley uses his hose and his water, he'll get a dousing of water where it will do the most good. He rejects Sturdley's denials, and repeats his threat. Late that night, you slip the end of Harry's hose inside a crack in Sturdley's car window, taking the usual care not to be seen. Set your alarm so that you wake up in time to watch the fireworks when Sturdley discovers his water-logged car.

Note that it doesn't have to be Sturdley's car; it can just as well be his basement window, or even his porch or living room window. It also doesn't matter if Sturdley discovers the hose before the torrent of water causes a flood. You can't measure the success of your instigation by raw physical damage. In other words, it's the thought that counts.

It helps to be very indirect when you create a situation from scratch. Use others to do some of your work for you. Even totally imaginary characters will do:

Pedro lives next to Harry Target. One night, you run the blade of a screwdriver or "church key" down the side of Harry's car several times. Next day, you commiserate with Harry when he wails over his ruined paint job, and mention that the same thing happened to your cousin the previous week. You add that your cousin had seen several Hispanics running from the scene. Your wife or accomplice mentions to Pedro's wife that Harry suspects that Hispanics put the scratches in his paint job, and that he hates and suspects Hispanics because he feels that they're dirty, sneaky people. That night, after making sure that everyone else is asleep, you put scratches on Pedro's vehicle. Just in case that doesn't get things going, the following night you slash Harry's tires.

Exploiting Political Correctness

Some companies have definite and identifiable corporate cultures, and employees who want to get along must conform. Non-conformity can result in being frozen out of pay increases, promotions, and bonuses. In some cases, non-conformity is a violation of company rules. Let's look at a few examples:

Some companies have "no-smoking" rules, both on and off-duty, although some states have now passed laws that forbid an employer from banning off-duty tobacco use. Still, if the corporate culture is anti-tobacco, a smoker or chewer will find himself frozen out socially, and even left out of bonuses and promotions.

Exploit this by planting a pack of cigarettes in one drawer of your target's desk. Another way is to put a cheap pocket butane lighter on top of his desk. Leave it to him to explain it's not his, especially when you plant another lighter on his desk whenever he's not looking. Yet another way is to place a pack of cigarettes on his car seat, where it may be noticed by fellow employees and supervisors. The best way, of course, is if you can obtain a jacket exactly like your target's, and put it in a room or closet full of tobacco smoke for a day or two. Bring it to work in a plastic bag so it doesn't air out, and substitute it for your target's jacket when you have the opportunity. With the jacket reeking of tobacco, you won't have to depend on someone "finding" a planted pack. If the company has a group health plan with different premiums for smokers and non-smokers, repercussions can be more serious.

Alcohol on the job is bad news, both because employers are concerned about deterioration of performance by employees with alcohol-fogged brains, and because of liability if the employee gets injured on the job. Planting a small bottle of liquor in your target's desk will raise eyebrows if anyone sees it. If there's an employee coat rack, one way to ensure that the word gets around is to buy small "airline" bottles of whiskey, and plant one in your target's coat pocket. However, first loosen the cap to ensure it leaks. Soon, the odor will be conspicuous, and will lead right to your target's coat, with the incriminating evidence right in the pocket.

Remember that exploiting political correctness by planting items on your target's desk can work for only a few times before he realizes that the incriminating items didn't get there by themselves. Planting material too early in the game can alert him to the danger, which illustrates that proper timing is everything. Introduced at the right moment, planted material can be very effective, because others will not believe that your target is a victim of foul play.

Attitudes and beliefs are not illegal, nor are they grounds for termination, under the law. However, there's a world of difference between statutes and the "unwritten law," and an employee who expresses, by word or action, attitudes foreign to the corporate culture can measure his future career with a stopwatch. This is the key to putting your target in the hot seat. There's an array of tactics that can make it appear that your target embraces attitudes offensive to the corporate powers-that-be.

While feminists claim that American business has a "glass ceiling" to keep women down, some female-owned companies have "lace curtains," which impose their own demands. Any male employee of a "lace curtain" enterprise has to watch his step. A *Playboy* or *Penthouse* magazine on your target's desk, for example, is evidence of the worst crime of all, "male chauvinism" that "exploits women as sex objects."

A bumper sticker with a slogan that's politically incorrect for that company's culture can be as effective. "Gay and Proud," and "Honk If You Love Jesus" are two strong statements guaranteed to offend somebody. So is a copy of Adolf Hitler's *Mein Kampf*. Fortunately, there's a wide variety of bumper stickers available at low cost. **Caution:** Don't use the bumper sticker tactic until your target's already being flushed down the toilet.

Confidential Papers

One good way to provoke a confrontation with an employer is to remove some confidential papers from the supervisor's office and place them on your target's desk. A day when your target is absent provides the best opportunity for this.

The next task is to let the boss know of the unauthorized possession. You might get a chance to tell him directly if the supervisor comments in your presence that he can't find the XYZ Report. You then say to him, "You must have lent it to Harry Target. He's got it on his desk." Unfortunately, this tactic depends on chance.

Another and more direct way lies open to you if you have legitimate reason for access to a particular confidential document. You say to your boss: *"I'd like to copy some figures from last month's production report. Can I borrow it from Harry's desk for a few minutes?"*

Another way is to have an accomplice tell the boss. This isolates you from the event. Yet another way is to pass the work to the office ass-kisser or company snitch. This has a three-fold effect. First, it gets your target in trouble. Next, it exposes the snitch to resentment and possible reprisal from your target if he finds out who snitched to the boss. Finally, it can provoke a confrontation between the target and the snitch, or even an uninvolved person.

If your target is slightly paranoid, he may suspect someone who had nothing at all to do with the affair of denouncing him to the boss. You can help this happen by mentioning "confidentially" to your target that Joe Brown-nose had a long discussion with the boss the day before.

Personal Property

It may be difficult to obtain a supervisor's confidential reports, especially if he keeps his office door locked or keeps the papers in a safe when not in use. However, you don't absolutely need access to confidential documents to put your target in the soup with his boss, because you can take advantage of the fact that many people strongly resent others borrowing their property without permission.

Next time you're in your supervisor's office, slip his desk lighter into your pocket when he's not looking. If he doesn't smoke, there are other personal items you can "borrow," such as a monogrammed pen, gold-plated letter-opener, etc. After you leave, drop the purloined item on your target's desk.

Exploiting the Snoop

Although it's incorrect to mention the topic in polite society, many offices have snoops and gossips. Some snoops go to the extreme of rummaging through fellow employees' desks or trash to find out what they can. This offers the perfect opportunity to start a rumor behind your target's back while remaining overtly aloof. A short list of items that can provoke malicious gossip follows:

- An employment application for another company, partly filled out and crumpled.
- A "draft copy" or "carbon copy" of your target's resume, recently updated.
- A publication going against corporate culture, such as a copy of *The Daily Worker*, or a copy of *Playboy* in a feminist-dominated business.

When exploiting the person addicted to gossip, it helps to have one or more accomplices. One of your accomplices can reinforce the "rumor" by stating it again to the gossip. Another can keep his ears open and report back to you if the rumor you instigated is circulating around the workplace.

The office gossip can become your inadvertent ally if you handle the situation deftly. The gossip thrives on rumors, and you can use this channel to spread damaging information and even "disinformation" anonymously.

Disinformation plants erroneous ideas in the target's mind, to mislead him and cause him to make serious errors. A program of disinformation can lead the target to making serious trouble for himself, and in a way that can't be traced back to you because he did it all to himself.

Let's scrutinize a few examples:

> *Harry Target and Joe McNasty are rivals for an impending promotion. You tell the office gossip "and keep this to yourself" that Harry was bad-mouthing Joe to the boss last week.*

Sometimes, a rumor alone can provoke a conflict. In other cases, you have to help it along. The opportunities are many:

> *You begin as before, telling the office gossip in confidence that Harry was carrying bad tales about his rival Joe to the boss. Two days later, your accomplice mentions that Joe is pretty burned off about Harry's unethical tactics. Two days after that, Harry finds his tires slashed.*

The most effective way to exploit office gossip is to tailor it to fit existing occurrences:

> *Harry and Joe are bitter rivals. One day, upon leaving the office, Harry finds that his car's been sideswiped in the company parking lot. You whisper in the gossipy person's ear that maybe, just maybe, a certain*

person might have had it in for Harry. Give your "spin"
on the situation a day or two to circulate, then put some
deep scratches on Joe's car with a screwdriver.

You can even use the gossip to sabotage your target by proxy and posthumously, so to speak. If you're leaving the company, and you know that your target's been hungering for your job, you can give your target a painful mental hot foot by telling the gossip that your boss confided in you that Harry would have the position as soon as your desk was vacant. You can only imagine Harry's poignant disappointment when the job goes to someone else, and he later discovers that he wasn't even in the running. Another example can take place if Harry's the one leaving:

Harry Target has found himself a better-paying job
elsewhere, and you're familiar with the company. You
know Mr. Savage, the plant manager, to be a very up-
tight and religious person who hates to hear profanity.
You spread the disinformation through your ally the
office gossip that the way to get along with Mr. Savage
is to tell him a dirty joke every morning.

You can even induce your target to sabotage his chances of getting a certain job by adroitly devised disinformation:

The gossip tells you that Harry Target is testing for
employment with XYZ Company, and you know that one
of the tests they administer is the Rorschach ink blot
test. You feed back to the gossip that your cousin, a
psychologist, had told you that the way to pass such a
test is to provide a lot of violent responses, such as
seeing guns, atomic explosions, dead animals, and
other blood and guts responses to the blots. You say
that businesses today seek aggressive personalities be-

cause they're go-getters, and that a pattern of aggressive responses will almost guarantee getting the job. This is precisely the wrong information, because a preponderance of blood and guts responses on the ink blot test presents a picture of psychosis. However, if Harry accepts this disinformation at face value and acts on it, he'll screw himself right out of the job. Furthermore, he'll have compromised his chances of ever being employed by that company, no matter how many times he applies, because test results often remain in personnel files for many years.

Yet another instance of disinformation depends on your acting upon several items of correct information, and may be hard for you to carry out. It's worth examining, though, because if you ever get the opportunity, you can deliver a devastating strike against your target:

You know that Harry's been seeking other employment, and you even know several companies where he's applied. You have an accomplice telephone Harry to say:

"This is Mr. Savage of the XYZ Company. I'm glad to tell you that we selected you for the opening. When can you begin?"

Believing that the job is his, Harry gives notice, and two weeks later, he's high and dry.

Note that some companies have become notorious for immediately terminating any employee who gives notice. Instead of letting him work out his two weeks, they have him escorted to the gate at once. The theory behind this is that the employee won't be giving his best with one eye on the door, and they're better off without his dubious services. Another rationale is that the departing employee will be packing proprietary information in his attaché case to take to his new job, and immediate termination reduces the risk of industrial espionage. Either way, Mr. Harry Target is out on the street, PDQ.

Door Slamming

A basic principle when leaving a company is to go gracefully, and "not to slam the door," because you may need their favorable reference one day. One deft way to induce your target to slam the door, and hard, begins with the same tactic:

Harry gets a call that he's got the job he'd been seeking. You know that there's been tension between Harry and Mr. Hardnose, his immediate superior. After Harry's given notice, he takes a couple of days' sick time. At this point, you tell the office gossip that you regularly pass the company that hired Harry on your way to work, and that this morning you noticed a car that looks very much like Harry's in their parking lot.

If Harry doesn't take any time off, you have to try another tactic:

After Harry's given notice, you or an accomplice ask him during lunch or break-time how he feels about getting out from under Mr. Hardnose's thumb now that he's leaving. Unless Harry's very restrained, those present will get an earful. If the office gossip wasn't on the scene, you can carry the news to him, and let it trickle down to Mr. Hardnose. If Mr. Hardnose is the least bit sensitive, sit back and enjoy the fireworks.

Even after Harry leaves, you can torpedo his chances of obtaining a favorable reference in the future, and totally close out any chance of his returning to that company. You and an accomplice discretly leak to the boss that Harry had had many unkind things to say about him while employed there.

Direct Action

This tactic requires one of two things:

- You're in very good standing with the boss, so that he'll accept your word without question, or:
- You have several accomplices within the company who work in conjunction with you.

Recruiting accomplices isn't hard if your target really deserves what he gets. If your target is a nasty, unpleasant, or treacherous person, he'll have created a backlog of unsettled scores. Fellow employees will almost be standing in line to have a go at him.

If you're working alone, wait until your target calls in sick. Go to the boss the next day and tell him that your wife saw your target at a shopping mall.

Alternatively, you can tell the boss that the target's wife called your wife and said her husband didn't make it to work because of a severe hang-over.

If you have partners in crime, you can be more exploitative. When there's an important meeting scheduled, one of your accomplices tells your target that the meeting's been canceled, in the presence of another in on the plot. When the meeting takes place, if the boss notices your target's absence, you sidle up to him after the meeting and say:

"Look, I may be speaking out of turn, but Harry told me he's sick and tired of attending these meetings. He said nothing gets done, anyway."

If the boss confronts the target, and the target replies he was told the meeting was canceled, there are two people who will testify that he was told no such thing.

e-mail

Working with your target produces many opportunities to sabotage his life. If you know your target's schedule, especially his roster of appointments, you can go on a rampage. E-mail is easy to forge when you want to embarrass the target, and even provoke confrontations. Unless there's an unbreakable security system in your office's e-mail, you can deposit messages "signed" by your target, or alter a genuine message written by him.

An example is a faked message canceling an important business meeting:

H. E. Gottrocks
Gottrocks Construction Co.

Dear Mr. Gottrocks:

I regret to inform you that I have to go out of town on Monday, the 18th, and cannot, therefore, meet you at your office to finalize the terms of the new contract. I'll have my secretary call you for a new appointment. Sincerely,

Harry Target

Another way is to change the time or place of the meeting:

H. E. Gottrocks
Gottrocks Construction Co.

Dear Mr. Gottrocks:

I would like to change the date of our meeting, as I have to go out of town on Monday, the 18th, and cannot, therefore, meet you at the Greasy Spoon restaurant to discuss the terms of the new contract. I'd like to meet you the following day, same time, at the Hung Low Chinese restaurant on 18th Street, and hope that this will be convenient for you. If not, please advise me. Otherwise, I'll see you on Tuesday the 19th.

Sincerely,

Harry Target

If the meeting was originally to take place at a restaurant, the target arrives but Mr. Gottrocks doesn't. If the meeting is scheduled at Mr. Gottrocks' office, your target shows up but Mr. Gottrocks isn't expecting him.

At this point, the multiplier effect may kick in to enhance the disruptive power of the gaslighting. If Harry Target is annoyed with Mr. Gottrocks for missing the appointment, he may confront him indignantly. Mr. Gottrocks, in turn, will wonder why Harry Target is blowing his top, as he's the one who changed the appointment. He may show the message changing the appointment to Mr. Target, who will deny he ever sent it. This may not sound acceptable to Mr. Gottrocks, who may conclude that Mr. Target simply forgot. If the argument becomes heated, the following consequences may ensue:

Mr. Target alienates one of his company's clients.

Mr. Gottrocks complains to Mr. Target's boss about his behavior.

Rumors begin to circulate that Mr. Target is losing his grip.

Sexual Harassment

While you have to watch your step if your target is female, the situation can turn if you handle it adroitly. There are several ways to put your target on the hot seat, facing accusations of sexual harassment. If your target is male, the basic tactic is to send notes and gifts to a female fellow employee. In some cases, your target will be your unwilling accomplice, if he has a reputation as a "ladies' man." Even without a reputation, if he's ever made a comment to another employee that he finds a woman attractive, his words will return to haunt him, and make his denials unbelievable.

Another use of e-mail is to write a romantic note to a female employee, signing your target's name. If the note is fairly explicit in its sexual language, and the woman is married, it can cause a stir. However, you don't need this combination of circumstances to make this tactic work.

With "sexual harassment" a hot and emotional topic today, simply sending romantic notes to a woman who doesn't appreciate receiving them will bring a charge of sexual harassment. Such an emotionally-laden accusation makes your target "guilty" until proven innocent. The effect will be explosive if the company is owed by a female, or staffed by a group of "feminists."

It's worth remembering that this tactic will work even if your office doesn't use e-mail. Simply typing a suitable note on your target's typewriter one day when he's absent will produce the same effect. Sending it in the inter-office mail, or simply dropping the note on the woman's desk, serves perfectly for delivery.

You can compound the effect of the trumped-up sexual harassment by making some anonymous phone calls. Once you deliver a note or two in your target's name to a female employee, begin calling her late at night, and breathing heavily into the phone. If the female recipient of the notes brings charges, it's even worse for your target. You continue the heavy breathing during late-night calls, and the obvious conclusion is that your target is the guilty party.

Nasty, Nasty

Some workplaces have no females. A variation on the sexual harassment tactic becomes necessary, and one is the homosexual note, in which your target makes an advance to a male staff member:

Dear Charlie:

Since you've come on staff, I've been impressed by how well you do your work, and by your charm and personality. I feel we should get to know each other better. How about dinner together at XYZ Restaurant tomorrow evening?

Anxiously awaiting your reply,

Harry Target

To make sure that there's no misunderstanding, the "XYZ Restaurant" mentioned in the note is a well-known gay bar.

Variations

Setting up your target for a sexual harassment charge is a very powerful tactic because it's workable in a number of ways, using high-tech or low-tech methods. You'll have the employer on your side, because no employer wants to face a lawsuit for allowing or condoning sexual harassment in his workplace. You don't necessarily have to write a series of notes. You don't have to have access to e-mail. All you have to do is have flowers or candy delivered to a suitable subject.

Some florists deliver, and you have an accomplice go to the florist to place the order directly, paying in cash. Using the telephone to place the order, and having it billed to your target's phone bill, doesn't work as well these days, especially if your area has "Caller I.D."

Florists provide gift cards with their floral arrangements, and your accomplice simply signs your target's name on the card. It doesn't matter if the signature is not an exact match, because it's extremely unlikely that the signature will ever be examined by a handwriting expert. The odds are great that nobody will believe his denials, even if the handwriting doesn't look like his.

The first bouquet has a signed card. After the female employee expresses her resentment, another bouquet arrives a few days later, with an unsigned card. The following week, a box of candy arrives via UPS, and next week brings a piece of inexpensive jewelry. Each present provokes a nasty response from the woman, or even her supervisor, if she's brought this to his attention. At this point, it doesn't matter if your target has denied ever sending the first bouquet, he'll have the can pinned onto him regardless. A few heavy-breathing phone calls can't hurt. In fact, the telephone is useful for many other tactics.

Telephone Games

E-mail isn't the only vehicle you can use. If you have a female confederate, she poses as a business contact's secretary, and telephones your target or his secretary, if he has one, to arrange or cancel appointments. The effects can be explosive in some cases. If an important client is scheduled to appear at a certain time, and your accomplice telephones to "cancel" the appointment, your target may be out of the office when the client shows up, which will cause an affront.

CB Games

Citizen's Band radio provides a perfect opportunity to provoke a confrontation between your target and a very aggressive person. You simply start an argument with someone on the CB, insult him, and state that if he wants to do something about it, you're prepared to face him down at any hour, day or night. If the person you're insulting is a nasty biker type, or worse, your target will be in real trouble.

When using this tactic, don't worry too much about involving an innocent person in your nasty little game. Remember, decent people don't accept challenges to fight from an idiot on the CB.

The Missing Report
and Other Choices

An office rival will sometimes try to sabotage an adversary's work by swiping a crucial report from his desk, but this trick is too well-known to work very well today. The only hope you have is if you know that your target has a rival, and will blame the report's absence on him.

One reason swiping a report doesn't work well is that most offices have computers, and the employees do their work on disks, producing a print-out only when they need a hard copy to submit to the boss. Therefore, swiping the paperwork won't do much damage, especially if your target has a high-speed printer that can produce another copy in minutes.

Instead, you can destroy the report's effectiveness, and make it a liability for your target, by altering some facts and figures in it. There are several ways to embarrass your target, and earn him a reprimand from his supervisor, by taking advantage of modern computers.

The first is to gain access to your target's computer and make the alterations directly. However, this may not be possible if your target has a security system on his computer, and has to enter a password to gain access to the files. Unless you know the password, you'll be locked out of access.

If you're a computer hobbyist, and have talent as a "hacker," you may devise a way to gain access without the password. Alternatively, you may discover the password, taking advantage of the fact that most people use their middle names, addresses, names of family members, or street addresses as passwords, because they're easy to remember. In fact, one computer expert listed a group of passwords that he stated are used 90 percent of the time.[1] Look up the list and use it as a starting point for breaking into your target's computer.

If your target's computer isn't a "stand-alone" unit, but is linked into other machines in the office with a local-area network (LAN), you may be able to gain access to his files from your keyboard. This allows you to "down-load" his report and make suitable alterations. Then you can print it out, and substitute it for the report your target submits.

Workplace Sabotage

Sabotaging your target's work is an excellent way of provoking a confrontation with his supervisor, but it's effective only if it appears to be the result of his carelessness. This is why setting fire to his work station is counter-productive. The same goes for deleting massive amounts of data from his computer. There are other and more subtle ways of sabotaging your target's work to make it appear to be entirely his fault:

- In a machine shop, exploit any break your target takes to alter the settings on his machine after he's set it up and passed first-piece inspection. Turning a knob, or changing the computer-control setting, can change a critical dimension by a couple of thousandths of an inch, enough to turn an entire lot of parts into scrap metal. Another way is to remove one part from the lot, making it appear that he spoiled it and discarded it to hide his mistake.
- Another tactic can have even more serious repercussions, because it involves another employee, and is only suitable if you have a reason to "get" both of them. Remove your target's micrometer or caliper and put it at the other's work station, or vice versa. This will inevitably result in an accusation of taking the instrument without permission, and if one or the other is hot-tempered, can produce fireworks.
- A delayed-action tactic along the same lines is to re-calibrate your target's micrometer or caliper, setting it to read one or two thousandths high or low. If your target's a conscientious machinist, this may not work well because he'll check his micrometer each morning with a "Jo Block," a precision-made block of stable metal used to calibrate instruments. The tactic you use then is to gimmick his Jo Block. Borrow it long enough to grind a couple of thousandths off one side, then polish it to a mirror finish to match the original surface. When he next uses it to check his calibration, he'll inadvertently set off the calibration of any instrument he checks with it.
- A quick and dirty way to produce the same effect can work if your target has only one calibration block in his toolbox. Simply substitute another of a slightly different dimension. It's very unlikely that he'll scrutinize the engraved number on it every time he uses it to calibrate his instruments.

- In a retail outlet, make an extra entry on his cash register. He'll come up inexplicably short in his tally at the end of his shift.
- Another way to alter his tally is to remove a refund slip from his drawer. If he's having a busy day, he may not even remember how many refund slips he put in, and at the end of the shift will be unable to account for the shortage.
- If you work in a service industry, swipe one work order from the stack on his desk or on his clipboard, to make it look as if he had lost it. He'll have to explain why the repair or work order wasn't performed.
- If you and your target work for the postal service, swipe letters from your target's bundle and drop them into an alley somewhere on his route. You may have to do this several times before a citizen reports the discarded mail to the post office, but when the ship hits the sand, it will hit hard! There are severe penalties for misdirection of mail. However, be prepared, in some locales, for some very apathetic citizens who wouldn't report it if their neighbor's house were on fire. In such a case, make an anonymous call to the postal inspectors.
- If your target is a photographer, open the back of his camera momentarily while he's not looking. You'll fog his film and he'll have several totally spoiled exposures to explain away. If you want to be more subtle, open his camera in subdued light, to produce a light fog. This will not obliterate the images, but will make them very difficult to print. Note that this may not work if he uses a modern electronic camera that automatically resets the exposure counter to zero when the back is opened. The counter will betray that something is terribly wrong.
- In a photo processing plant, surreptitiously add acid, such as sodium sulfite, to your target's developer. This is particu-

larly effective with a film or paper processing machine, because it will degrade the quality without making it too obvious that something's gone wrong. Add very little acid to the replenisher, and the effects will be slow in coming. Worse, as he adds more replenisher to compensate for decreased activity of the developer, he'll only aggravate the problem. Only a chemical analysis, highly unlikely under the circumstances, will disclose this form of sabotage.

- In a custom photo processing laboratory, go into your target's darkroom during his lunch break and flash several boxes of printing paper. Don't make it too obvious. Expose the paper just enough so that it will turn a very light gray.

- If you both work in a high-security plant that requires an employee badge to enter and to leave, swipe his badge just before quitting time, putting it in a place where he logically could have dropped it. If you do this on a day you know he has to be home early, he'll be frantic while trying to find it.

- Some high-security companies have access controlled by "card keys," magnetic-striped cards that open locks and gates. If you have even momentary access to your target's card-key, wipe a powerful pocket magnet over the stripe, the same technique that negates ATM cards. Your target's card will suddenly become inoperative, with annoying results.

- In a hospital, opportunities for workplace sabotage are endless, but it's necessary to use fine judgment to avoid any harm to innocent persons. One harmless way to indict a hospital employee responsible for paperwork is to remove the consent for surgery or treatment from a patient's chart after the treatment has taken place. For legal reasons, consent slips are essential in hospital practice, and the absence of a consent slip after major surgery causes severe concern.

- If you don't have time to rummage through a chart to remove a couple of papers, make the whole thing disappear. Losing a chart is a major black mark for any nurse.
- A charge nurse with the keys to the narcotics cabinet has full responsibility for its contents. If the opportunity arises, removing some of the contents and disposing of them in the garbage can cause a major investigation, with inevitable repercussions against the nurse. Just make sure you appear totally uninvolved.
- Fast-food outlets offer several opportunities for sabotage. If your target cooks hamburgers, leave a box of frozen patties out next to his grill. The supervisor will see them and admonish him that taking patties from the freezer long before cooking makes them spoil.

The Job-Seeker

Many employers take an uncharitable view of a staffer's seeking other employment, viewing this as blatant disloyalty. As we've seen, a few interpret it as such a serious affront that they'll fire summarily any employee who gives notice. In any case, an employer considering one of his employees for promotion will reconsider upon learning that the employee is job-hunting. Take advantage of this by "framing" your target as a job-hunter.

The simplest way to do this is to have an accomplice, unknown to the target's employer, telephone his supervisor:

> *Good morning, I'm Jack Frost, personnel manager at the XYZ Company, and I'm calling to verify Mr. Harry Target's employment with your firm.*

Another way to do this is to take advantage of the situation if your target's mail is opened by his secretary or in the mail room. You use a purloined letterhead from another company to write a letter thanking your target for appearing for an employment interview, and telling him that he'll be notified shortly whether he has the job. Office gossip being what it is, it's almost inevitable that the news will spread. The reason?

If his secretary doesn't like him, she'll be happy to spread news that will hurt him. It may be even worse if his secretary does like him, and has a strong feeling of loyalty towards him. In such a case, she's bound to feel hurt that her boss didn't confide in her, and her feeling of loyalty can easily turn to loathing.

What if your target doesn't have a secretary? What if he opens all of his own mail? You can still make this work, using at least two other methods.

The first is to type the same letter, and mail it to yourself at home, addressing the company envelope in pencil. This is to get a canceled stamp on the envelope. Upon receiving it, you open the envelope, erase your name and address, and type the name and home address of your target. You then put the letter back in the open envelope, throw it on the floor, and step on it a few times to scuff it.

The next problem is getting someone in your company to read it. Some people who pick up open envelopes are tempted to read the letter inside. You can test for this by bringing an innocuous letter addressed to yourself to work and dropping it on the floor, with a hair folded over the letter inside the envelope. When someone returns it to you, check to see if the hair is still in place. If not, Bingo! That person has read your letter, and it's reasonable to suppose that he will read any other letter he finds. It's especially helpful if this person is your target's rival or supervisor. Next morning, take the forged letter in to work with you and drop it where the same person is likely to find it.

Another way to get the forged letter in front of the supervisor's eyes is to photocopy it, and send it anonymously through the office mail, or simply drop it on the supervisor's desk. You can kill two birds with one stone if your target's rival has printed memo pads saying, "From the Desk of Johnny Rival." You swipe a few sheets, and have your accomplice, whose handwriting is unknown at your company, print the supervisor's name on one sheet, then staple it to the forged photocopy.

Yet another way to put your target neck-deep in the soup is to fill out an employment application for another company in his name, if you can forge his writing or printing reasonably well, and leave it on his desk one day during his absence. An alternative tactic is to photocopy it and send the copy anonymously to the boss, with an unsigned note saying:

> *"Look what Harry Target had on his desk the other day."*

Don't forget to mail out résumés in your target's name to a number of companies, especially those where the owner or one of the executives knows your target's supervisor. Word will leak back.

The fake job search can also sabotage your target's home life. Letters from companies arriving at home can provoke a lively discussion between your target and his wife, who will demand to know why he hasn't confided in her that he's job-hunting.

If by chance you discover that your target is really looking for another job, this will provide the opportunity to hit him with a series of sinister gut-punches, to torpedo his chances of being hired. As pointed out in the first chapter, the more you know about your target, his aspirations and interests, the better your chances of carrying out an effective gaslighting campaign.

Put together a list of the most likely job prospects for him. Include jobs advertised in the newspapers, but don't forget companies in a similar line of work. Prepare an outrageously fictitious résumé that's sure to attract negative attention. One

Gaslighting

90

way to sabotage his prospects is to list a totally fictitious last
job. When the company's personnel department checks his
background, the last job listed is the one getting first attention.
Another point is to list phony educational attainments. Let's
look at the way you might do it for a target seeking employment
as a shipping clerk:

RÉSUMÉ

Harry Target
309 Jones Street
Punkintown, USA
Age: 39
Married, two children
Health: good.

EMPLOYMENT HISTORY:
 1989-1994: Purchasing Agent for General Motors Corp.
 1987-1989: Production Manager for General Dynamics Corp.
 1980-1987: Eastern Marketing Manager for Ford Motor Company
 1974-1980: Sales trainee, then sales manager, General Specialty Corp.

EDUCATIONAL HISTORY:
 1970-1974: Harvard Business School, Graduated, M.B.A.
 1966-1970: Brown University, Pre-Med Major
 1962-1966: Benedict Arnold High School, New Rochelle, New York,
   Academic Major, Class Valedictorian

HOBBIES AND INTERESTS:
 Member, Socialist Worker's Party, Students For A Democratic Society.

Go to the copy machine, run off a hundred or so copies, and
send one to each company on your list. Be generous and give
every possibility the benefit of the doubt. Don't bother forging
your target's name to a covering letter: the résumé will be
enough.

Two weeks later, follow up with a telephone call to each company on the list. Giving your target's name, ask why they haven't replied to him. Be forceful at first, then become abusive. Sprinkle the conversation with profanity, especially if you're speaking with a woman. Lace your diatribe with phrases such as "dumb broad." Even a woman with no interest in feminism will take offense if you attribute her alleged stupidity to her sex. The more nasty, vulgar, and abusive you are, the more vivid an impression you'll make, ensuring that your target's name will be remembered if he ever applies to that company for employment.

The Cheating Heart

If your spouse, "Nancy," is cheating on you with your best friend, this is both bad and good news. The bad news is the crushing sense of betrayal that will fall upon you like a ton of bricks. The good news is that your easy access to both will provide an excellent opportunity to provoke severe anxiety by exploiting disinformation. Once you form an idea of how long the affair's been going on, you can plan your approach.

During planning, remain on good terms with both your wife and your "best friend." However, the plan has a built-in safety factor if you lack the total self-control you need to disguise your feelings. In one respect, you'll have to have a lot of emotional fortitude, because this devastating plan requires you to tell a very damaging lie about yourself, while delivering a devastating mind-burn.

Begin by allowing enough time, at least a year, to pass between the beginning of their affair and the moment you act. At the appropriate moment, take your "best friend" off to a quiet corner:

You: *I guess you may have noticed something's been on my mind during the last few months.*

Best friend: *Yeah, I noticed you haven't been yourself lately. You seem to have something serious on your mind.*

At this point, your target's guilty conscience may suggest to him that you've discovered his betrayal and are about to confront him. This produces enough anxiety so that he'll accept your next statement with a profound sense of relief, and because you're confessing to him, with total credulity.

You: *I guess you never suspected this, but I'm gay. I don't think Nancy knows, either, but since before we were married, I've been seeing this guy, and we've been having sex at least once a week.*
Friend: *(shocked) No, I never knew.*
You: *Well, it's worse than that. My buddy Charlie also goes to bars, and he's been picking up guys for one-night sex. About two years ago, I had a routine check-up and my blood tested positive for HIV. So Charlie never told me he had it.*
Friend: *HIV? Have you told Nancy?*
You: *No, I didn't have the guts. If I told her I'd gotten HIV, I'd have had to tell her the whole story, and I couldn't bring myself to do that. I know she's got it, because you don't test positive until months after you get it, and by that time, you've been contagious for a long time.*

If you want to lay it on thickly, you begin crying, repeating that you've murdered your wife with the virus. This is maudlin, but a very easy story to believe.

This conversation leaves your best friend wondering about his status, and trying to cope with not having sex with your wife again to avoid catching AIDS, if he hasn't already been infected. If he's married, he will wonder if he's spread it to his wife, and if his wife's pregnant, the complications become mind-boggling and terrifying.

This isn't a male-only technique. Wives also sometimes have to cope with a close friend carrying on an affair with their husbands. A similar tactic works against an unfaithful husband and the wife's close friend. If your husband's cheating with your neighbor and best friend, and she is married, here's one possible approach. Next time you and your neighbor are having coffee together, the conversation may go like this:

She: *I went to the doctor last week, and he called me yesterday to tell me I'm pregnant.*

You: *That's very good news! I know you and Joe have wanted a child for a long time.*

She: *Yes, I'm finally pregnant, and I just wonder how long it'll be until I know if it's a boy or girl.*

You: *I don't think I'll ever get pregnant. We decided not to have any children because Harry's got a Down's syndrome gene in his make-up. His brother had a boy with Down's syndrome, and we don't want to risk going through that.*

At this critical juncture in the conversation, you may notice your neighbor and best friend become pale, as she considers the implications. When having regular sex with two or more men, it's impossible to be absolutely sure who the father is, as even the best methods of birth control aren't 100 percent certain. She'll blame your husband, her lover, for not telling her of this genetic deficiency, although she may not confront him. She'll also have to face the difficult decision of whether to have the child and risk bringing forth a mental defective, or to have an abortion. If she chooses abortion, how will she justify this to her husband?

Making this work properly requires careful preparation on your part, to make it credible. Genetic disorders vary with ethnic background, and you have to survey the latest research to find the disorder that fits your husband's ethnicity best. Blacks are vulnerable to sickle-cell anemia, while Jews tend to inherit Tourette's and Tay-Sachs Syndromes. Know your facts before you act.

The Loan

Another way to use disinformation to bash your target in the chops is to plant faked "news" about a loan application. Obviously, you have to be close enough to your target to know the details of his plan.

If your target tells you of his intention to buy a house, you can deftly elicit some critical details. You need to know if he has to give his landlord written notice of his intention to vacate the premises, the name of his mortgage company, and the date of the application.

With this information, you recruit an accomplice whose voice your target won't recognize, and who telephones him posing as an agent of the mortgage company. He informs him that his application's been approved, and that closing can be within 30 days. Your target, elated by the news, gives his landlord notice, and when he discovers the hoax, will find himself out on the street if his apartment has already been rented.

You can do the same with an auto loan, although this won't cause your target as much dislocation as the fake home loan approval. Although many banks and auto dealers today have instant approval for loan applications, your target may apply to a company that takes longer. If so, he's wide open to a disinformation scam. If you know that your target plans to sell his present vehicle privately, a fake call telling him his auto loan has been approved can move him to advertise it for sale. At the very least, he'll waste time showing it to prospective buyers before he's prepared to sell it, assuming his loan application eventually goes through. If he accepts a deposit, he'll be obliged to sell it, however inconvenient it may be.

The Ladies' Man

If your target is a ladies' man, follow him when he goes out on a date. If he takes his date into a restaurant, theater, or any other establishment where you can have him paged, have a female accomplice pose as his "wife" and telephone the manager's office and request the manager to page your target, citing an emergency at home to give it urgency. The beauty of this tactic is that it works whether your target is actually married or not. His date will be shocked to discover that he has a wife somewhere. The other nice aspect of this is that it works against female targets as well.

One possible problem with this tactic is that paging can be very discreet, with a simple announcement stating: "Will Mr. Harry Target please come to the manager's office?" This doesn't disclose the reason, and can fall flat.

Throwing Gasoline on the Flames

Creating a conflict between your target and another person takes a fine hand, but it can often be even more productive to exploit and aggravate an existing one, when a little effort can go a long way. The basic tactic is to do something to further antagonize one of the parties, in a way that although your target knows he didn't do it, he won't be believed if he denies it. Obviously, timing is everything. Let's examine several scenarios to see the opportunities and to lay out tactics and timing appropriate to various situations:

Gaslighting

> *Your target has become involved in an argument with his boss on a controversial social or political issue, such as abortion. The supervisor is pro-abortion, and your target is a right-to-life advocate. Ever alert to the ramifications, you place a bumper sticker on the supervisor's car. The sticker reads: "Abortion is Murder." Guess who the principal suspect will be when the boss sees what's on his bumper?*

The bumper sticker tactic is for when you don't want to do any physical damage and the owner of the vehicle can take effective reprisals. You can also use the bumper sticker tactic as a follow-up to a situation you've created, such as parking your target's car in the supervisor's parking place. If you can't obtain the proper bumper sticker quickly enough, other tactics are possible:

> *After your target has had a confrontation with his boss, you go to a pay phone late at night and ring the supervisor's number. When he answers, say nothing and let him hang up, then call him again in ten minutes. Keep this up most of the night, changing locations after the second call and each subsequent one to negate tracing by the telephone company. You'll immediately know if your tactic is successful if you hear the person you're calling begin cursing out your target and threatening to settle accounts at the office the following day.*

In other situations, you have to be more forceful:

> *Your target, a salesman, is involved in an intense rivalry with another salesman, and has just accused the other of raiding his territory and pirating some of his customers. You have reason to dislike both, and decide to act quickly before the incident blows over, by slash-*

ing the tires of the other salesman. Obviously, your target is the prime suspect, leading to more trouble. If you want to take this a step further, the next night you slash your target's tires. Meanwhile, you have a female accomplice telephone your target's clients for appointments, posing as the rival's secretary. The news will quickly get back to your target.

This can easily lead to a fist-fight, or worse, so you have to be sure you want to involve the other party to this extent, and not bring harm to an innocent person.

Similar tactics work when there's a neighborhood dispute. As usual, you must be prepared to take immediate advantage of every fleeting opportunity:

You overhear your target telling of a dispute with his neighbor, who repeatedly parks his car with one set of wheels on the target's lawn. Late that night, you go to your target's house, and if the offending car's parked half-way on his lawn, you flatten the tires. The neighbor will blame only one person, and it won't be you!

Exploit other opportunities as well:

Your target lives in an apartment, with a neighbor who plays his stereo or TV too loudly, and repeated complaints have produced no satisfaction. That evening, you go to the location, and if you hear the sound turned up loudly, go to a pay phone and call the neighbor. Scream "Turn it down" at him, so loudly that he can't be sure the voice is not the target's voice. Then go back to the apartment and throw a brick through the neighbor's window. Of course, the neighbor will storm out of his apartment and begin banging on your target's door, and the fun will begin.

There are several possible variants on this scenario. One is based on the concern that you might be seen running away, or that the neighbor might pursue and catch you. The way to cope with this is to telephone the neighbor during the small hours of the morning, screaming, "Now I'll keep you awake!" and throw the brick through his window once you see the lights go out again. Still another way is to catch the neighbor asleep when you throw the brick, to be sure of getting away before he becomes fully awake and gets on any clothing. You can telephone him afterward, and threaten that the next time you'll use a bottle of gasoline. When police arrive, you'll have been long gone.

If the dispute involves an animal in any way, you can take advantage of the road-kill we so often see on our streets:

> *Your target's dog has bitten a neighbor's child. This is serious enough as it stands, but you want to add to the problem. Late one night, throw a dead dog onto your target's door-step to be found in the morning. This silent act is sure to be perceived as a threat by your target.*

With enough such episodes, neighbors may begin to perceive your target as a crank. You can, of course, help the process gather momentum.

The Neighborhood Crank

Once your target has begun to lose credibility with his neighbors, a few more efforts will build a reputation as the neighborhood crank. The basic tactic is a series of unfounded complaints. Note that it will be very helpful if your voice sounds like that of your target. If not, make a serious effort to find an accomplice who can mimic your target's tone and accent. The results will be devastating.

If your target has his newspaper delivered, call the newspaper's circulation office a couple of times per week, giving his name, and complaining that his newspaper never arrived that morning. It helps to be abusive. If the route manager arrives with another copy to replace the missing one, and sees it at his door, it won't take long for your target to become known as a nut case at the newspaper office.

You can make this work even if your target is an early riser and takes in his paper as soon as it arrives. Simply telephone the circulation office before the time you know he awakens, and complain that the paper isn't there yet. It's almost certain that the staffer who answers the telephone will reply that they don't consider a delivery missed until 6 or 7 A.M., but you remain completely unreasonable, and insist on getting your paper RIGHT NOW!

If you or your accomplice sound like your target, telephone one of his neighbors late at night and complain about the loud music. If you refrain from making the call until you've seen the neighbor's lights go out, the person will be peeved at having been awakened to hear a spurious accusation.

The next tactic works only if the local police do not have a 911 system, similar to "Caller I.D.," that displays the caller's number on the operator's screen. From a pay telephone, call the police to complain about your target's neighbor's loud music. A few such unfounded calls and the police will consider him a crank too. This can have very beneficial side-effects by destroying his credibility if he ever calls the police to complain that someone is doing things to him.

If the police have a caller display system, you can still make this tactic work if you have a spare handset and the skill to tap into your target's line. Thus, any call you make this way will display as coming from your target's number, and you can make crank calls to the police almost at will. The only restriction you must observe is to do it when you know your target's not using his telephone, so that he won't hear the extra voice on his line.

Notes

1. *Computer Viruses, Worms, Data Diddlers, Killer Programs, and Other Threats to Your System*, John McAffee and Colin Haynes, NY, St. Martin's Press, 1989, pp. 89-91.

Chapter Six
REAL TROUBLE

There are several ways to place bureaucratic booby-traps designed to cause your target serious trouble, legal and otherwise, in his immediate environment. For these tactics, it helps greatly to have access to your target's wallet, home, vehicle, and mail.

Missing Papers

State law usually requires a motor vehicle operator to have with him not only his driver's license, but the vehicle registration and, in states with mandatory liability insurance, the vehicle's insurance certificate or card. If ever your target leaves his vehicle unlocked, or if you have access to it another way, such as "borrowing" his keys, just remove the registration form and insurance card from the glove compartment. People don't normally check to verify that their registration and insurance paperwork are in the vehicle each time they get in the car, and the next time your target gets into an accident, or is stopped by a police officer, he'll get a citation for not carrying the required paperwork with him in the vehicle.

The Fake Drivers License

Access to your target's wallet allows the simplest of these tactics. Simply borrow his drivers license long enough to make a same size Polaroid photo of it, and return the fake to his wallet.

The Polaroid Corporation makes several same-size copying attachments, the simplest of which is a close-up lens. This is good enough to produce a copy that will appear real to casual inspection, such as when your target flips through the credit card envelopes in his wallet. However, if he has to use the card as credentials, such as when making a purchase with a check, or show it to a police officer, the fake will stand out like a sore thumb.

The reason? State drivers licenses are designed to resist forgery. Some have a fine network of lines printed through the photo, and others, such as New Mexico's drivers licenses, have a stamped lettering of the state's name that appears when holding the card at a certain angle. Yet others have a logo that does not reproduce when photographed. Presenting a forged drivers license to a police officer will produce serious repercussions, even if the motor vehicle bureau's computer verifies that your target has a valid license.

The Fake Registration

Making a vehicle registration slip that is an obvious copy or forgery takes even less equipment. Once you borrow the real registration from your target's vehicle, make a photocopy on an ordinary copy machine, and return the copy to the vehicle. A police officer will be able to spot the copy, because it will lack the colored validation stamp, which reproduces in black on a copy machine, and your target will have some explaining to do.

You can guarantee results by a simple extra step. Using white-out, obliterate one of the license plate numbers on the registration before making the copy, then slip the copy into your typewriter and type in another number or letter. A police officer will immediately notice that the registration and plate do not match, a fact which will be verified when he calls in for a check with the state motor vehicle bureau computer. Then the ship will hit the sand.

An even better way is to intercept your target's application for a new registration, and mail back to him a fake of your own making. The plate numbers match, and even the envelope is real, as you've saved the one in which your registration arrived. You won't be able to supply a validation sticker for his plate, but your target may think this was merely an oversight by a clerk in the motor vehicle bureau. If he doesn't pursue this, feeling secure because he has a valid (he thinks!) registration certificate in his glove compartment in case he's stopped, he'll find out differently the first time a police officer stops him.

The vehicle registration will have lapsed, and he'll become aware of it when the officer ominously orders him out of the car, possibly even at gun-point. If the officer stopped him for drunk driving, his fate is sealed. He's going to jail, because the combination of DUI and a fake registration will leave the officer no choice.

One possible problem is that your target may notice that his check to the motor vehicle bureau never cleared his account. This omission, while it would alert a normally functioning human being that something, somewhere, has gone wrong, may pass completely unnoticed, because by the time you get to this stage, your target will already be suffering mind-damage.

The Stolen Car

One way to guarantee that your target's vehicle will come to the attention of the police is to report it stolen. You don't need access to your target's telephone for this. Simply call from a pay phone at a shopping mall, and state that your car disappeared while you were inside the mall.

Fake Hunting License

You can perform the same sort of forgery with a hunting license. Intercepting your target's application and substituting a forgery by return mail will cause him a pack of trouble when a game warden asks to see his license.

Forgery Tips:
Making Real-looking Fakes

With official documents carrying several security features to frustrate forgery, you have to be able to produce a fake that looks good enough for casual inspection, but will surely show up as a fake in an official inspection. Polaroid photography is good enough to produce an acceptable drivers license, so that your target won't notice it's not real.

If the forgery is too crude, even your target, dull, brutish and insensitive as he may be, will notice something wrong with it. A little care goes a long way. What you need is a forged document that won't scream "fake," so that your target's hunting buddies don't begin wondering why his hunting tag is printed only in black.

First, try to duplicate the real document's color, texture, and stiffness as closely as you can. If the drivers license is laminated, pass your Polaroid forgery through a plastic laminator.

If you're faking a vehicle registration printed on ordinary bond paper, use similar paper to make your copy. A color stamp can cause a special problem, because color is one of the most conspicuous attributes on the face of a document, and a black-only imitation will stand out too much to pass unnoticed.

Some copy machines, such as the Canon PC6-RE and several Minolta models, use toner cartridges, and the manufacturer sells cartridges with color toners for those who want to copy in color. This copier's instruction manual even describes how to produce two-color printing on one sheet of paper. This merely requires removing the colored part of the document from the black original to avoid printing it in black. Making the colored image requires pasting the colored stamp in the same location on a white sheet of paper, changing the toner cartridge, and running the copy through a second time. Two passes, and you've got your realistic forgery.

Your target's problem will occur because the numbers printed on the forgery are fake, and will not pass inspection. They won't match his vehicle's plate, or VIN, and the officer will become very inquisitive.

You can help this along while making your Polaroid photograph of his drivers license by altering his registration or license number. Type a few fake digits on an oblong piece of white paper and lay it over the real number while photographing it. A police officer scrutinizing the license will immediately pick up on the disparity, and a radio check will confirm it.

An important point regarding detecting forgery is mind-set. Police officers are aware that some people travel on falsified papers, and they routinely double-check with the computer to verify the status of the document. Your target, on the other hand, won't be expecting a fake. After all, he just sent in his money to pay for a license, registration or insurance card, and he's legally entitled to one. The one he receives in the mail has to be real, because a state agency sent it. This mental factor works for you whenever you substitute forgeries in his wallet or glove compartment.

Plate-Swapping

A quick and dirty tactic, if your target has two vehicles and you cannot gain access to his keys, is to swap the registration plates. Most people don't check their license plate numbers each day, and as long as they see a plate where it's supposed to be, that's enough for them. However, it won't be enough for the first police officer to stop either vehicle, because the plate and registration won't match.

Don't swap plates with a vehicle belonging to an innocent person. You don't want to cause anyone uninvolved with your target problems.

Bad Checks

One way to cause mind-bending and aggravating problems, including criminal charges, for your target is to issue bad checks in his name. This does not involve forging checks from scratch, but signing his name to genuine checks drawn on an account with insufficient funds.

The first step is to obtain his account number from discarded deposit slips, canceled checks, or by simply copying it out of his check-book. Practice signing his name, until you can produce a reasonable facsimile. Next, you go to another branch of his bank far from his home or workplace, where it's unlikely that he's known by sight. You open a second account in his name, depositing a minimal amount of money. Use a mail drop to receive the printed checks.[1] When they arrive, you're ready to go to work.

If you have access to his incoming or outgoing mail, pay some of his bills using the new checking account. If you can get hold of his outgoing mail, open the envelope flaps with a wet sponge and remove his check, substituting your own. The checks will bounce, of course, and your target will find his utilities cut off, and perhaps his car repossessed and his bank accounts taken over by the Internal Revenue Service.

Luck can play a part, as well. If you're lucky enough to find a starter check-book in a dumpster or elsewhere, use those for paying your target's bills. As starter checks are for temporary use, only until the printed checks arrive, many people discard a partly-full book upon receipt of the printed checks. This saves you the trouble of impersonating your target.

Eventually, the truth will come out in the wash, but the time this takes appears infinite to the person being pursued by creditors, who simply don't want to hear any stories or any statements except "Here's your money."

Contraband

Remember the illegal drug and the handgun you obtained a long time ago, for use in a certain contingency? Well, here are several ways you can use them to put your target in very deep doo-doo.

If your target's on his way to the airport to catch a flight, and you get the opportunity to slip your untraceable handgun into his briefcase, the airport security system will do the rest. Once his handgun shows up on the X-ray screen, he'll have so much explaining to do that he'll probably miss his flight, even if he doesn't suffer immediate arrest.

If you know that there are drug-sniffing dogs in use at this airport, sprinkle the small amount of illegal drug you've saved in his pants cuff or jacket pocket. He will find himself detained and searched by airport police after the drug dog "alerts" to the odor of the drug on his person.

If your target is going to visit a relative or friend in state prison, this provides an opportunity to employ any of several tactics. The typical state or federal penitentiary has one or more signs at each approach, which read something like this:

STOP!
WARNING!

You are entering prison grounds. It is absolutely forbidden to bring any firearms, ammunition, alcoholic beverages, illegal drugs, or other contraband onto prison grounds. If you have any such materials in your vehicle or on your person, do not proceed beyond this sign. All vehicles and all visitors are subject to search, and anyone found in possession of contraband will be arrested.

Place a handgun under one of the seats in your target's vehicle. If you weren't able to obtain an untraceable handgun, use the illegal drug. Lacking even this, put a bottle of booze under his seat or in his glove compartment. You don't even have to spend much money on the liquor. A small airline-size bottle will appear very incriminating, because its small size makes it very concealable, ideal for smuggling into a prison.

To make certain that your target and his vehicle will receive the scrutiny they deserve, make an anonymous telephone call from a pay phone. Describe your target and his vehicle, even providing the license plate, and tell the prison administration that Harry plans to break out his brother Bill that afternoon. The authorities will do the rest.

Snitching Him Off to the Cops

One way to cause real trouble for your target is to inform the authorities of any illegal activity in which he's involved. In most cases, it's perfectly possible to inform anonymously, as police agencies operate "hot lines" for anonymous tippers. In some cases, especially those involving illegal drugs, there's even a reward for information.

However, it's possible to snitch him off even if he's walking the straight and narrow. An unfortunate fact of American life in the Twentieth Century is that some agencies operate as loose cannons, conducting arrests and raids on meager evidence, or even no evidence at all. The instance of the Bureau of Alcohol, Tobacco, and Firearms in Waco, Texas, is too well-known to warrant discussion here. The main point, however, is that the Waco incident wasn't unique: it was only the best-publicized because of its extremely violent nature and large casualty count.

BATF Agents raided the home of a Toledo, Ohio, man after receiving an anonymous letter that he was involved in a "White supremacist plot." The "plot" allegedly was to bomb a predominantly Black public housing project, but federal officers admitted in court that they had no evidence to support this allegation. Agents did not identify themselves as law officers when they broke in, and the man opened fire at them, but was acquitted of the charge of "aggravated menacing" by a jury.[2]

This instance wasn't unique. U.S. Drug Enforcement Agency (DEA) officers have raided the wrong premises, and some local agencies have even planted narcotics to be "discovered" during a raid. The fact is that some law enforcement officers, and the agencies employing them, are "hot dogs" who will do anything to make a bust, and will make an arrest or apply for a search warrant on little or no solid evidence. This provides an opening for you if you decide that your target deserves a visit from the cops.

An anonymous letter is the best way to go. When composing your letter, be as specific as you can, even if you have to fabricate facts or slant them to suit your case. If, for example, you know that your target goes to the movie theater every Tuesday night, state that he meets his drug wholesaler at the theater. Officers surveilling him will note that he does, as stated in your letter, go to the theater each Tuesday night, and they'll draw the conclusion you want from this confirmation of your allegation.

Protecting Yourself

Obviously, forging official paperwork, stealing your target's mail, and writing checks in his name can cause serious repercussions for you if you're caught. You may end up in worse trouble than he, and you'll wish you had never begun.

This is why it's better to be safe than sorry. If you have any doubts about your security, abandon that phase of your plan and concentrate on the parts that don't expose you to risk.

Regarding risks, let's examine them, and note a few ways to counter or minimize them. In carrying out some of the more aggressive tactics, such as opening a checking account in your target's name and purloining his mail, you run the risk of being identified and of leaving fingerprints. There are ways of reducing these risks almost to zero.

Let's tackle the easy one first. Always wear plastic gloves when handling anything that you're going to send in your target's name. If you forge a letter, write a check, or redirect mail, never handle these items bare-handed.

Be especially careful when handling mail. Remember that the U.S. Postal Inspection Service is a low-profile but extremely proficient law enforcement agency, better than their peers. Over the years, their conviction rate has been higher than the other two well-known federal agencies, the FBI and the Secret Service. You surely don't want the Postal Inspectors on your case.

Identification is another problem. Obviously, don't be seen lifting envelopes from his desk or entering his home. Reducing the risk while opening a checking account is more difficult because you have to show your face, and you may even have to show some identification.

There are two ways to ensure that a bank clerk won't be able to identify you. One obvious way is to wear a disguise. This doesn't mean a total cosmetic make-over, but a simple disguise, designed to obscure part of your face. If you're normally clean-shaven, wear a false mustache. If you don't wear glasses, put on a pair for the occasion. Of course, always wear a hat, to obscure your hair color and style, but don't wear the type of hat you normally wear. If you like baseball caps, wear a captain's cap or a fedora. Better yet, if you've bought a hat of the sort your target wears for the size-switching tactic, wear that, if it fits your head, to complete the disguise.

The other aspect of impeding recognition is time. Open the fake checking account long before you plan to use it, as a witness's memory fades with time. Months or a year later, the bank teller who served you won't even remember the incident.

Finally, you may have to show identification. This isn't likely if you already have a deposit slip or can provide the number of your target's current account at the bank. Bank personnel pay closest attention to people trying to withdraw money, not deposit it, and this reduces the scrutiny you'll receive.

If push comes to shove, however, and the teller insists on seeing identification, reach for your wallet, and exclaim with surprise that you must have left it at home. Excuse yourself with a promise to return the next day, and vanish forever.

Notes:

1. *How to Use Mail Drops for Privacy and Profit*, Jack Luger, Loompanics Unlimited, Port Townsend, WA, 1988.
2. *Gun Week*, October 22, 1993, p. 2.

Chapter Seven
A FINAL WORD

Now that you've examined the variety of gaslighting techniques available, you can choose those that will work best against your target while exposing you to the least risk. Always remember that not all techniques work in all situations. The name of the game is "survival," so don't take unnecessary chances. Choose carefully, to allow you to enjoy your target's discomfort and deterioration.

Seeking A Final Solution

In the beginning, gaslighting proceeds with a light touch, allowing you to take it as far as you wish. Later, many direct gaslighting tactics are forceful and discrete, for use when your target's on the way down. They are the equivalent of sinking a ship and machine-gunning survivors in their life-boat. Which you choose to employ depends on what you feel your target deserves.

YOU WILL ALSO WANT TO READ: